$1/-

The Woman Who Ate CHINATOWN

The Woman Who Ate CHINATOWN

A San Francisco Odyssey

Shirley Fong-Torres

Author of *IN THE CHINESE KITCHEN*

and *SAN FRANCISCO CHINATOWN, A WALKING TOUR*

iUniverse, Inc.

New York Bloomington Shanghai

The Woman Who Ate CHINATOWN
A San Francisco Odyssey

iUniverse books may be ordered through booksellers or by contacting:

iUniverse
1663 Liberty Drive
Bloomington, IN 47403
www.iuniverse.com
1-800-Authors (1-800-288-4677)

Because of the dynamic nature of the Internet, any Web addresses or links contained in this book may have changed since publication and may no longer be valid.

The views expressed in this work are solely those of the author and do not necessarily reflect the views of the publisher, and the publisher hereby disclaims any responsibility for them.

With special thanks to photographers Frank Jang and Kenny Wardell

ISBN: 978-0-595-44867-8 (pbk)
ISBN: 978-0-595-69037-4 (cloth)
ISBN: 978-0-595-89191-7 (ebk)

Printed in the United States of America

To my father and mother

TABLE OF CONTENTS

FOREWORD

When Shirley asked us to write a foreword to her new book, *The Woman Who Ate Chinatown*, we were honored, yet nervous. It is difficult to capture in words a dear friend whose professional culinary career spans more than three decades and who has contributed so much to the color and culture of our Chinese community.

Two years ago, when we heard rumblings of Shirley's new book about Chinatown in San Francisco, we knew it was going to be something special and a book only Shirley could write. After all, she has lived and breathed Chinatown for the better part of the last twenty plus years, following the tragic loss of her older brother Barry during Chinatown's turbulent days. Her initial query into his death turned into a lifelong preoccupation with the inner workings of a community that sometimes is really an inner city within what most see of San Francisco on the surface. Shirley's tragedies and triumphs are interlaced with her daily touches about the community that essentially is her real life backyard.

From the years of knowing Shirley, one gets a sense that she has taken on the strong, diverse character that is also the spirit of her personal Chinatown. She is at once most generous with her feelings, but also intensely protective of her proud values whenever affronted. Above all, one cannot ever forget meeting Shirley for the first time. Her immediate, infectious smile and laughter warms nearly everyone she touches. This book will most certainly touch you as if you are with Shirley in person—she is guiding you through Chinatown and has cooked you a fabulous meal.

We have known Shirley closely for the last seven years now, but it might as well be decades. Shirley brings sunshine into the kitchen even on dreary, difficult days. Once her magical personality touches you, as it has us, you will be led into a world where goodness always seems to prevail. On many occasions, Shirley would drop into our restaurant, Shanghai 1930, when all seemed to be in tatters, but somehow her smile and presence always made us feel that everything would turn out fine. She and Wro (her fabulous honey bear) would mosey up to the bar and order martinis—and you, who needed to laugh, would thank God that *Shirley was in the house*.

With all respect, we must also acknowledge her brilliance in presenting the culture and cuisine of our native China and neighboring environs. We have never met anyone who was such a natural in front of the camera, especially doing live shows. She would hack a chicken and tell jokes while focused on the task at hand of preparing a recipe to the finest detail. These culinary skills, of course, are honed from many years of training and teaching, and her technique comes so naturally, we think Shirley could teach an ape to cook well. Although Shirley toyed for many years with the idea of owning and operating a restaurant, fate would have it that she shines best in the kitchens of her many friends. As we can attest, the glamour of owning a beautiful, seemingly successful restaurant does not hide the many hours of intensive labor and heartache required of this intrinsically difficult business.

Although Shanghai 1930, our main Chinese restaurant, is not located in Chinatown, Chinatown was the real enclave where new immigrants coming to America gathered for more than a century. Here, restaurants representing flavors from home could be had without venturing outside the comforts of immigrants' new "home." This is where Chinese dialects were spoken and people tended to follow similar practices and lifestyles. Chinatowns across the country became symbols for the American immigrant experience and later even became a tourist attraction in major cities, as many Occidentals had not had the chance to visit real China until recently. San Francisco's Chinatown was *the* most famous of all Chinatowns in America and perhaps the world. In the 1850s, the immigrants from southern China flocked here to San Francisco during the Gold Rush and were major contributors in building the railroads and in mining. Most of these folks made their homes in San Francisco's Chinatown and added to the flavor of the city—although it was not their choice necessarily, as "Chinamen" were restricted to certain areas. Shirley's many explorations and personal discoveries in this book will give the reader an insight into those early years and the transformation that has occurred in the hundred plus years since the conception of Chinatown.

Shirley's many insights and anecdotes are cleverly captured in this wonderful book, but never think that this work is the lonely imagination of a celebrated culinary writer. The chapters illustrate the rich and diverse history of Chinatown through the years as witnessed by Shirley herself. Her famous Wok Wiz Chinatown Tours have shown thousands of visitors and locals alike the real history and flavor of Chinatown. These Wok Wiz walks, often led by Shirley herself, can take on a life of their own as if the walls of Waverly Street or Grant Avenue were speaking to you directly through Shirley. Lastly, the book is a wonderful, informative guide—not just about Chinatown; it also speaks luminous volumes of the immigrant experience that has seldom been so colorfully chronicled. Like many of us in the first few generations coming to America,

Shirley Fong-Torres speaks proudly and personally of this experience and the strength of diversity that makes America great.

Cynthia Wong-Chen and George Chen
Owners of Shanghai 1930, San Francisco

INTRODUCTION

Hi, my name is Shirley Fong-Torres and I will be your writer tonight. Our special is San Francisco's Chinatown, handcrafted by an obsession with good food and tossed with a reduction of personal and historical anecdotes.

Since I own a walking tour company in San Francisco and conduct culinary tours all over the world, my career demands that I eat, talk, and evaluate food. I think about food almost all day long. When I try to engage my food-friends in other subject matters, it is no surprise that the conversation goes back to food. For instance, "Have you seen the new exhibit at the Baltimore Museum?" "Oh yes, and they have this fabulous café, you must try it!"

First things first; I am Chinese, not Hispanic. And long-time *Rolling Stone* senior editor, writer, and radio personality Ben Fong-Torres is my talented brother. I am asked about that so frequently, I thought it would be a good idea to introduce him right away.

Me with my brother, Ben Fong-Torres
(Photo by Kenny Wardell)

Here is how we got the hyphenated surname. From 1882 until 1943, the Exclusion Act made it nearly impossible for Chinese to come to the United States. My father, Fong Kwok Shang, was born in 1903 in the Hoy Ping district of Gow Bay Hong in Guangdong, China. At age eighteen, he made a decision that would forever change his life. To improve his life, he wanted to move out of his village, get a job elsewhere, provide for his family, and then return home one day. He heard that there were job opportunities in Manila, so he moved there and landed a variety of jobs. Dad would work all day at one place and then help out in a Chinese restaurant for several hours. He sent some money back home to his family in Gow Bay Hong, but it was not enough. He wanted to follow some of his friends from the village to the United States, but the Exclusion Act of 1882 was still in full force. What to do, what to do?

After six years in Manila and saving as much money as he could, he learned that the only way he could leave was to pretend he was a citizen of the island. For $1,200 he was able to obtain a birth certificate that stated he was Ricardo Torres. Now he had a ticket to ride. In the 1960s, new laws allowed Chinese like Dad to admit they were "paper sons" and become legal citizens without penalty. Father did this so that each of his children could have a Chinese surname. He added his true last name, Fong, and hyphenated his fake last name to make up the Fong-Torres surname. We grew up in Oakland and spent a great deal of time in Dad and Mom's restaurants. Today's Silver Dragon is only a block from the original one that Dad owned, when it was called the New Eastern Café.

In the span of his culinary life, Dad left California to open a restaurant in Reno, Nevada, with my brother Barry in tow to help him, and Ding How in Amarillo, Texas, where he took then twelve-year-old Ben along. Dad was also a chef at the first Trader Vic's for a few years. Dad's last restaurant was the Bamboo Hut in Hayward, California.

Mother came to this country in 1940, selected as my father's bride by relatives in China. She was a "picture bride," as Dad saw a picture of her before she came to America to marry him. My mother was born in 1921 in a small village not far from my father's. My grandfather, whom I never met, was a school-teacher, and my grandmother held a variety of jobs while raising her family. At age eighteen, my mother sailed to America to begin her new life.

My mother and father's wedding portrait.

My father, in front of the Ding How restaurant in Amarillo, TX, 1956.

I cannot remember a time in my life that I do not associate with foods. As a little girl, I played and napped in the "rice room" of our restaurant. Our sister Sarah taught me how to dance to radio music among hundred-pound bags of rice. Coincidentally, *The Rice Room* is the title of Ben's award-winning memoir about growing up in Oakland's Chinatown and later becoming the senior editor of *Rolling Stone* magazine. Sometimes between American school and Chinese language school at the Chinese Community Center, Ben and I treated ourselves at a nearby restaurant to steaming, fresh Chinese roast pork buns—*char sil bows*. On occasional afternoons, Dad and I dropped by the coffee shop next door to our restaurant, where he would order a cup of coffee and a slice of custard or apple pie. I did not order anything because Dad always saved the best part for me—the crust.

When our father and Ben moved to Texas to operate Ding How, I was about ten years old. The rest of the family remained in Oakland. I still remember hearing my mother's voice: "*Seung Nui, sai mai.*" That is how she summoned me to wash rice. In Cantonese, *sai mai* translates to "wash rice," and *Seung Nui* was my Chinese name. I heard that so often, I thought that "wash rice" was part of my name.

Mother's cooking often fascinated me. Even before my rice-washing days, while Dad and Ben were away, I spent hours watching and helping her cook. I recall her delicious steamed egg custard with bits of Chinese sausage; soups with all sorts of Chinese herbs; heavenly sponge cakes; and, on rare occasions, roast spareribs and potatoes, which was a huge treat for us. Mom also made wonderful Lunar New Year dumplings and other savories.

Another childhood memory places me in the kitchen of the original Trader Vic's on San Pablo Avenue in Oakland. I remember sitting in the kitchen of Trader Vic's nibbling on a snack, later to be named crab rangoon, that Dad made for me. Dad was one of the first chefs at the original Trader Vic's. Now, crab rangoon is served in restaurants around the country and it pleases me to know that it was created at Trader Vic's.

By the time I was a teenager, my father and mother had opened the Bamboo Hut in Hayward, California. My brothers and I were obligated to help out at the restaurant after a day in public school. Because I took the bus all the way from Oakland High School, Dad almost always had a bowl of *won ton* soup waiting for me, dabbing just a drop of rich, aromatic sesame oil to scent the broth.

My brothers and I managed to do our homework between waiting on tables and mundane chores like peeling prawns, wrapping *won tons* and egg rolls, making paper-wrapped chicken, mixing mustard, and making pots of what we then considered was coffee. It was often boring to be stuck in the restaurant while our friends were living typical teenage lives. So for fun, we would make one pot of coffee in the morning and then add water to it all day long. Sometimes we would dilute the coffee right in front of our customers' eyes. We were still kids, so maybe the customers felt sorry for us; I do not recall ever hearing complaints about lousy coffee or terrible service. For entertainment, Ben and I played the radio, forcing our customers to listen to our favorite music while dining—The Beatles, The Rolling Stones, Bob Dylan, Jefferson Airplane, the Temptations, Petula Clark. We had no idea then that Ben would one day interview all those singers for *Rolling Stone* magazine.

Before long, I was transferred to the kitchen. Perhaps my approach to customer service was not up to par? I was given more cooking-related responsibilities, helping my father at the wok station. I remember mixing gravy for his stir-fry dishes and learning how to make stock. Not only did I peel prawns, I learned to slice them and prepare them for deep-frying. Soon I was cooking alongside my father, observing more than anything. It was far too many years later before I appreciated that those were cooking lessons, and that my father was the best teacher I ever had.

Bamboo Hut closed its shutters about the time I was preparing to graduate from college. I taught physical education and English at Loretto Academy in El Paso, Texas, and spent eight years at Levi Strauss & Co. in San Francisco, hooked on discount jeans.

You can take the girl out of the kitchen, but you cannot take the kitchen out of the girl. In 1985, without any investment funds, I formed Wok Wiz Chinatown Tours, and have been showing people the culinary and cultural delights of Chinatown ever since. Often I have been asked, "How did you manage with no business loan?" I always believed that if you want something, you dedicate yourself to it, maintain the passion, work hard, and the rest will come naturally. Today, I have an extraordinary team of tour leaders who help me spread the word about our colorful, historical neighborhood.

The Wok Wiz Team at Shanghai 1930. From the left, first row:
Hank Quock, Shirley, Chuck Gee, Baby Stella with Tina Dong Pavao.
Second row: Rhoda Wing, Alberta Chinn, Lola Hom. Back row: Bernice Fong, Howard
Teng. Not shown: Dorothy Quock and Judy Won (find them elsewhere in the book!)

My personal favorite tour is called "I Can't Believe I Ate My Way Through Chinatown." I have discovered that for anyone who loves food and has a taste for adventure, it is the best way to absorb Chinatown. On this particular tour, we "eat history" as I tell stories about the early Chinese and how their survival and evolution depended upon food knowledge—using the sun, salt, and even dirt to preserve fish, shrimp, and eggs. Chinese vegetables were hung out, along with laundry, to dry. Chicken and duck eggs were preserved in salt water or dirt.

We start with a typical Chinese breakfast of *jook,* rice congee. When I talk about a certain food from the old days, more likely than not the guests will taste it on the tour. I have met way more than three thousand food lovers, have snapped countless pictures of my new friends trying "thousand-year-old eggs," bitter melon with beef, steamed pork hash with salt fish, salt 'n pepper Dungeness crab, and claypot with soy bean curd sticks and chicken. My goal is to introduce foods that I have eaten since my childhood, foods that have been in the Chinese diet for hundreds, even thousands, of years. Today, those foods still appear on kitchen tables and restaurant menus.

Eating dim sum on the street is fun.

In my travels around the world, I have visited many food museums—the Museum of Spam in Minnesota, the Mustard Museum in Wisconsin, and the Museum of Parmesan in Italy. I have enjoyed the hands-on experience of Iowa's living history farms and have explored food markets with chefs in Bali, Thailand, Prague, and Hong Kong.

One morning, before dawn at the Honolulu Fish Auction, it occurred to me that such a working segment of the food cycle is the best kind of food museum. Suddenly I had a new perspective on my twenty-three years of guiding people through Chinatown. I knew then that I had to write this book, so that I could enlighten all the visitors who will dine with me, have already shared a meal, or have spent an entire day of eating with me. In Chinatown, no foods are consumed in vain. Every single calorie can be an educational experience and a communion with our venerable ancestors.

I was born near Chinatown, grew up in Chinatown and some folks might say I am Chinatown crazed. After guiding visitors through San Francisco's Chinatown the last twenty-three years, I think I have consumed the spirit and history of the place along with nearly every dish our numerous restaurants and tea houses serve. An old adage says that all history is a conjugation of the word "to eat." Because of discriminatory laws, Chinese food was just about the only part of our culture assimilated by the rest of America. Today, Chinese food is still the most accessible means for visitors to Chinatown to learn about our ancient ways. So after decades as both a food writer and a Chinatown story-teller, I decided to combine those things and serve up Chinatown as an historical feast.

Although I grew up in Oakland's Chinatown, I have come to love San Francisco's Chinatown so much that I have consumed it both literally and metaphorically. I have eaten its food, its history, and its culture. In this book, I will take you to some of the places that are offered on my tours and invite you to join me in feasting on the history and culture of San Francisco's Chinatown. We will begin at Portsmouth Plaza and eat our way through 150 years as I tell stories about the early Chinese and how their survival depended upon food knowledge. Near the end of the book, we will visit my hometown, Oakland's Chinatown. Then I will share some of my favorite recipes with you. So, come with me now and get ready to taste the fruits of knowledge.

How to Get to Chinatown

San Francisco is a city that has great public transportation. Our compact city experiences traffic congestion and parking difficulties. This is especially true in Chinatown. Although it is enjoyable to visit any time of the day, Chinatown is much less congested in the mornings or late evenings. We start most of our Wok Wiz tours in the mid-morning. We use Portsmouth Plaza as the point of reference in these directions.

Walking from Hotels

Many of the guests on our Wok Wiz tours walk from major hotels in the city. Union Square is about eight blocks from Portsmouth Plaza, the "living room" of Chinatown. To walk from Union Square, go east to Grant Avenue, turn left on Grant, and you will enter Chinatown. If you want to go to Portsmouth Plaza, just walk down Clay or Washington and you will run right into the Plaza.

Most of the hotels near Fisherman's Wharf are about twelve blocks from Portsmouth Plaza. Ask your hotel concierge to direct you to Columbus Avenue. Follow Columbus until you see the business signs in Chinese—welcome to Chinatown.

Mass Transit

An excellent way to get to Chinatown from many points in the Bay Area is on BART, the Bay Area Rapid Transit system. If you have a car, drive to the nearest BART station, park there for the day, and avoid the stress of traffic. Many local bus systems feed into BART. For information on BART, e-mail www.bart.gov.

The BART station closest to Portsmouth Plaza/Chinatown is the Montgomery Street station. From this station, walk one block west to Kearny Street, make a right turn and walk six blocks, then go up Clay into Portsmouth Plaza/Chinatown. Other buses that pass by Chinatown are the new T-Third light rail line, the 9X line, and the #30 line (the drop-off is on Stockton Street). These buses also connect to the Caltrain system from and to the South Bay and the Peninsula. The Caltrain station is on Fourth and King, a block away from the AT&T Park, home of the San Francisco Giants. For further information, contact www.sfmta.com or call 415-701-4500.

Driving and Parking Tips

Consider www.mapquest.com or your favorite online map for driving directions.

- Hilton Financial District (located at 750 Kearny) is most convenient because the Wok Wiz daily tours begin in its lobby. The hotel offers a weekend rate of $3.00 an hour.

- Portsmouth Square Plaza, which is located directly across the street from the Hilton Financial district, charges $2.50 an hour. Visit their Web site to get information for a cool merchant validation discount for up to two hours of free parking: www.portsmouthsquaregarage.com.

- Golden Gateway Garage (located at 250 Clay Street, between Front and Davis, at the Embarcadero Center) offers validated parking for $3 (as of 2007) on Saturdays and Sundays until 9:00 PM. Google the Golden Gateway Garage San Francisco to get details on businesses that validate the parking ticket.

- On Sundays, try your luck at getting FREE parking on the street, if you come early and have the Parking Space Angel looking out for you. Of course, never park where it says "No parking seven days a week" or in any red zones. San Francisco has graphic signs directing tourists to Chinatown.

From the San Francisco-Oakland Bay Bridge

Take Highway 80 west to San Francisco. Take the Fremont Street exit, veer left onto Fremont, then left on Howard to Third Street, which becomes Kearny after you cross Market Street. On Kearny, stay in the left lane if you want to enter the Portsmouth Plaza parking lot between Clay and Washington Street, or go left on Washington to drive into Chinatown.

From the North/Golden Gate Bridge

Take Highway 101 south to San Francisco, and take the Downtown exit to Lombard Street, to Van Ness Avenue. Turn right onto Van Ness. Make a left turn from Van Ness onto Bush Street, and follow Bush to Grant Avenue to get into Chinatown, or go one more block to Kearny to get to Portsmouth Plaza and its underground garage.

From San Jose/South Bay using Highway 280

Take Highway 280 north to San Francisco. Take the King Street exit. Stay in the left lane to make a left turn onto Third Street, which becomes Kearny after you cross Market Street. On Kearny, stay in the left lane if you want to enter the Portsmouth Plaza parking lot between Clay and Washington Street, or go left on Washington to enter Chinatown.

From San Jose/South Bay using Highway 101

Take Highway 101 north to San Francisco. Then, take the Highway 280 exit towards Daly City/Port of San Francisco; continue on I-280 north towards the Port of San Francisco, and to San Francisco. Take the King Street exit. Stay in the left lane to make a left turn onto Third Street, which becomes Kearny after you cross Market Street. On Kearny, stay in the left lane if you want to enter the Portsmouth Plaza parking lot between Clay and Washington Street, or go left on Washington to drive into Chinatown.

From Fisherman's Wharf Area

Take the cable car to Chinatown. The cost is $5 per person, so it can get expensive. Ask your hotel concierge how to obtain a cable car pass, and you can ride merrily all day long for one set price.

Take the Powell-Hyde line (PH) or the Powell-Mason line (PM). The PH line is located near the Ghirardelli Square at Beach and Hyde Street. The PM line is located at Bay and Taylor Street. Get off at Washington and Mason (near the Cable Car Museum, on the corner) or Powell and California. Walk down a few blocks and you will be in Chinatown.

CHAPTER 1
HISTORICAL APPETIZERS

PORTSMOUTH PLAZA

In the days when Mark Twain and Robert Louis Stevenson hung their hats here, Chinatown's Portsmouth Plaza was one block from the infamous Barbary Coast. Everything between Montgomery Street and the Embarcadero was then under San Francisco Bay, so I like to think that Chinatown rose from the sea.

The Chinese were originally allowed to live in but a few blocks, so streets were named for their commercial specialties. Maps were less reliable than noses—the original Global Positioning Systems. Residents could pinpoint all locations by their proximity to Salt Fish Alley. Today, it is called Wentworth Alley, located kitty-corner to Portsmouth Plaza.

Salt Fish Alley was a key part of Chinatown's food district before the 1906 earthquake. Two of my tour leaders, George Mew and Hank Quock, tell me that their families operated salted fish and salted shrimp stores in this alley, starting around 1895. The salted shrimp and fish were first processed up on the rooftops with the help of the sun and a seasoning of salt. The aroma drenched areas even beyond the ally. Live fish, meanwhile, floated merrily in street-level tanks until they met their demise. Long before sun-dried tomatoes hit the food scene, the Chinese used the sun to preserve food, including fish, shrimp, and vegetables such as *bock choy*. The salt fish, *hom yee,* is still very popular, especially in one of my favorite dishes: Salt Fish, Chicken, and Tofu in a Claypot.

Most of the Chinatown fish and other seafood markets are now found up the hill on Stockton Street, but we will talk about that after lunch. For now, our destiny requires a stop at the legendary Sam Wo (located at 813 Washington).

Sam Wo restaurant, with the Transamerica Pyramid looming on the left.

Just about anyone who grew up in this area during the 1950s and 1960s has an Edsel Ford Fung story. Edsel was the animated, uncensored waiter who made Sam Wo famous. He had command of the second and third floors of the restaurant, while his brother Henry Ford Fung worked the first floor. Sam Wo's food was not its main attraction—customers came to see and be verbally abused by Edsel. He instructed customers where to sit and what to order. He did not necessarily bring you what you ordered, which he sometimes scribbled down while smoking a cigarette. If he was busy and you wanted mustard, either you would not get it, or he would take it from customers at another table, even if they happened to be using it. He was notorious for flirting with gals, rudely criticizing customers, and reminding people about tipping him. Yet customers kept coming back, especially with visitors from out of town. Immortalized in Armistead Maupin's novel and movie, *Tales of the City*, Edsel is still so fondly remembered here that our new AT&T Park named a concession stand after him. He would not be impressed or happy. They misspelled his last name.

Sam Wo occupies a narrow building, three floors high, with some eight tables on each floor. I prefer the third floor where the best way to get service is to shout down the chute of the dumbwaiter. I also shout up the chute to let the server know that I have arrived with my hungry tour group. A poster on the wall reminds guests "What to do in case of CHOKING." I don't know about you, but just knowing that such information is available stimulates my appetite.

After entering, you walk past the dumbwaiter and the kitchen area to get into the upstairs dining rooms. Sam Wo's *jook* is rightfully popular. This traditional Chinese breakfast is a rice congee that can be ordered with pieces of a thousand-year-old egg, raw fish, and less exotic things like lean pork. The Chinese bread, *yow jah gwai*, also known as *yow tui*, is a good accompaniment. Another nice side dish is *cheung fun*, stuffed rice noodles similar to a Japanese sushi roll. Prices are bargains, so despite the almost non-existent customer service, people still love the place these many years after "Edselisms" went out of production. My theory is that most folks feel compelled to return to test their sensory perceptions: the first time around, they really can't believe what they think they saw and heard and tasted.

In May 2007, Conan O'Brien taped a part of his nationally syndicated, late-night show at Sam Wo and gave it free on-air coverage for five nights. My good friend, photographer Frank Jang, went to eat there a couple of days that week and reported that the food remains "not good." I showed up for breakfast with a new group of "I Can't Believe I Ate My Way Through Chinatown!" diners, and the chef barked, "Come back later!" So, customer service is back to its norm.

Since the breakfast at Sam Wo did not happen, I discovered the New King Tin restaurant (located at 826 Washington, directly across the street from Sam Wo). It has excellent and tastier *jook*; I think the chef adds short grain rice to the *jook* pot to give it a creamier texture.

After the morning meal, it is best to take in a little Chinatown culture as a digestive aid. That means walking to Portsmouth Plaza, the birthplace of San Francisco. I am invariably greeted by the regulars there as they pause to say good morning to me. I love to teach our visitors, especially students, how to greet the Chinese on the streets or in the shops of Chinatown. It always brings smiles to the folks in Chinatown—it makes them happy to know the kids have taken time to learn a few Chinese words and sayings. Children, and kids at heart, learn how to say "*Nay ho,*" which means "How are you?" or "*Joy gheen,*" which means "Until we meet again." We also often greet one another with "*Sig may ah?*" which translates to "Have you eaten?" If you have not eaten, your friend will suggest dining together; if you have eaten, your friend will suggest having coffee, tea, or dessert. There is always a reason to eat!

Teacher Matt Pavao (the tall man), tour leader Hank Quock, and a group from Cabrillo School are in Portsmouth Plaza, ready for a Wok Wiz tour.

Birth of the City

The first Anglo-Saxon settler in this city was the English whaling ship captain William Richardson. On June 25, 1835, Richardson pitched a tent at what is now the heart of Chinatown, 827-43 Grant Avenue. A few months later, he built a permanent wooden structure, often referred to as the first house built on the site of the future city of San Francisco. Richardson became the port commissioner for Mexico, of which California was still a part, and collected taxes and tariffs for the Mexican government. Years later, he received a land grant for what is today's Sausalito, north across the bay. Once a refuge for tax evaders from San Francisco, Sausalito now receives tourists by both car and ferry.

From sunrise to sunset, Portsmouth Plaza is the hub of Chinatown's social life. There are few other parks in America where you encounter so many people in such a small area. Folks of all ethnicities and ages gather here, but the older Chinese men and women consider the plaza their de facto community center. In mid-2003, there was a noted change at the plaza. Dozens of primarily older women began asserting themselves on the male prerogative, congregating to play card games in the afternoons, much like their male counterparts had for a century or more. Although most of the women do not interact with the men, they have taken over one corner of the park, squatting or sitting on makeshift cardboard seats wherever they can find space.

As the morning opens, you may observe men and women practicing *tai chi*, a graceful and peaceful form of meditation and exercise. Throughout the day, seniors sit on benches to gossip, laugh, and relax. Children giggle and frolic in a playground of sand boxes and swings, under the watchful eye of parents, grandparents, and care providers. Groups of older women often gather with bags or boxes of Chinese take-out from nearby restaurants or cafes. They chatter about where they purchased fresh Chinese vegetables or fruits in season, and may peel back a sweet tangerine or two to share. Retirees spend their days outdoors here after years of hard work. Younger fellows relax with friends before going to work in predominantly food-related businesses. Board and card games predominate across ages, as does the study of the morning horse racing form, which is usually accompanied with tea and Chinese pastries or *dim sum*. *Dim sum* is a meal made up of a variety of steamed and fried dumplings, rice enclosed in lotus leafs, braised eggplants, stuffed tofu, and much more. A *dim sum* menu can showcase over a hundred offerings and is always served with tea. Sometimes we call *dim sum* "*yum cha*," which translates to "drink tea," which means it's time for *dim sum* and tea!

Portsmouth Plaza is an ideal place to enjoy your lunch or snack. I often see children of all ages nibbling on *char sil bow*, Chinese steamed or baked pork buns. When you purchase take-out food, ask for a pair of chopsticks or a plastic fork so you can join the crowd at the plaza and enjoy a meal in the sun.

Sittin' on the Dock of the Bay

Portsmouth Plaza faces north toward the towering Financial District. The Transamerica building is just one block away. I believe the office buildings guard Chinatown and that the "Money Gods" are watching over us. But that is a very new Wok Wiz-inspired story. For most of San Francisco's history, if you were sitting in Portsmouth Plaza, you were "Sittin' on the Dock of the Bay" (the song Otis Redding wrote about San Francisco). Montgomery Street, one block north of the plaza, was the infamous Barbary Coast, the shoreline strip of taverns and less-reputable establishments that dominated the city's image back in the post—Gold Rush days.

Portsmouth Plaza has been spruced up, thanks to the building of a new social center on the Kearny Street level and a playground for kids on the upper level.

Next to a modern elevator, there is an inviting rest area, complete with a Chinese-style pagoda roof. The four-level parking garage directly beneath is still one of the best and most affordable places to park in Chinatown. The garage's car entrance is on the street level of Kearny. After you park your car, get into the elevator, push the *P* button, and you can ride straight up to the heart of Chinatown.

Take a moment in front of historical statues honoring Captain John Montgomery and author Robert Louis Stevenson. Novelist and poet Stevenson lived here with Fanny Osbourne, whom he married in California. They resided on Bush Street from 1879 to 1880. That was the period between his writing of *Travels with a Donkey* and *Treasure Island*. He loved to sit and look at the ships out on the bay, and became a friend of the Chinese people, which was unusual back then. The friendship led to the creation of a monument to Stevenson, located at the northwest corner of the plaza. The ship on top is a replica of the *Hispaniola*, from *Treasure Island*, which may have been on his mind when he sat here. The inscription on the statue is from his book *A Christmas Sermon*. In his great ballad, "The Song of Rahero," Mr. Stevenson waxed obsessively about fish. Biographers have said he became the fisherman character Teriitera, so it is reasonable to speculate that the great writer watched the fishmongers carry their catch from the docks a block away, and that he probably purchased their seafood for his dinner.

At Portsmouth Plaza, a playground for children and a gathering place for locals and visitors, the Financial District "Money Gods" watch over us.

EARLY DAYS OF CHINATOWN

It is time to take a stroll before breakfast's second course, which I call breakfast dessert. After all, we must nibble on something every now and then as we "eat Chinatown."

Timing is important. At 10:00 AM, my friends at the Golden Gate Bakery (located at 1029 Grant Avenue, 415-781-2627) will be taking batches of perfect custard egg tarts, *donn todd*, out of the ovens. Along with moon cakes, melon cakes, almond cookies, and homemade pastries, these famous custard tarts have turned this bakery into the most sought after in Chinatown. Come early, as the bakery is popular and lines can be long. Another great place for fresh custard egg tarts is the Dick Lee Pastry Shop, located at 716 Jackson Street. The price is considerably less than at Golden Gate Bakery, but the flavor's right up there.

Memories of Portsmouth Plaza and the First Cable Cars

When my mother arrived in San Francisco in 1940, Portsmouth Plaza was dirty and dilapidated, basically a vacant lot with very few trees. It was not landscaped as it is today. Wok Wiz tour leader Dorothy Quock, recalls those days: "When I was about six years old, I tagged along with my brothers here to shine shoes, charging five cents. Sometimes the Caucasian customers paid my brothers and gave a few cents tip to me as well!"

In the 1970s, the bridge to the Chinese Cultural Center in the Holiday Inn (now the Hilton Financial District) was built as an urban renewal project. The Chinese Cultural Center offers exhibitions, lectures, and art by Chinese Americans. Its small gift shop has a good selection of books and souvenirs.

After the June 4, 1989, Tiananmen massacre in China, the *Goddess of Democracy* statue was placed in Portsmouth Plaza. The statue is dedicated to those who strive for and cherish human rights and democracy. There is also a plaque that marks the site of the first public school in California, built in 1847 and opened the following year.

On the Clay Street side of the lower level of this park, a bronze plaque commemorates Andrew Halladie, inventor of San Francisco's famed cable cars. Halladie had a wire rope manufacturing business on Powell Street, and his product was used with mining equipment for pulling carts up out of mines and other work. One rainy day in the winter of 1869, Halladie witnessed a horse-drawn cart accident and decided that there had to be a better way to get up our steep streets and hills. The answer came on August 2, 1873, when the first cable car line ran from Clay Street west up to Nob Hill.

Some days, I stand at the plaza and close my eyes to visualize what it might have been like for the Chinese people who may have wondered where those magical cable cars were going, up those hills to places where they were not welcomed. Coincidentally, one of my father's first jobs upon arrival in San Francisco was at the Fairmont Hotel on Nob Hill. He was able to get a job as a busboy by posing as a Filipino. However, he was not comfortable in that environment of wealth and luxury. I imagine that it must have also been very taxing for him since he was posing as a Filipino. If he spoke Chinese, his true identity would have been exposed and he would have been in a heap of trouble. Once he heard that a Chinese community was developing in Oakland, he quit his job at the Fairmont and made his way across the bay.

If you would like to learn more about the cable cars, I recommend that you visit the Cable Car Museum (located at 1201 Mason). Their Web site is www. cablecarmuseum.org.

Judy Won, right, leads a group of happy visitors through Portsmouth Plaza on a Wok Wiz tour.

Walter U. Lum, Chinese Activist

On the west side of the Portsmouth Plaza, a narrow street is named after Walter U. Lum, the renowned Chinese American civil rights leader, newspaperman, and first president of the Chinese American Citizens Alliance. This is the first street in the United States named after a Chinese person. Born in 1882, the son of a Chinese shopkeeper, Lum helped reorganize the Native Sons of the Golden State, which subsequently became the national Chinese American Citizens Alliance. In 1913, Lum and his fellow activists campaigned successfully against a constitutional amendment in California that would have deprived Chinese of the right to vote. In the 1920s, the Citizens Alliance lobbied Congress to revise the Exclusion Act to allow wives of Chinese citizens into the United States. Lum also served as a reporter for *Young China*, a newspaper of Sun Yat-sen's Chinese Nationalist Party, and in 1924, Lum became editor of the *Chinese Times*, the first Chinese-language paper in the United States whose mission was to serve Chinese Americans. This tireless advocate for his community died in 1961, and his efforts will always be remembered. On April 26, 1985, the name Brenham Place was officially changed to Walter U. Lum Place.

At 7 Walter U. Lum Place, there is another Asian American civil rights organization, Chinese for Affirmative Action (CAA). Since 1969, CAA has been promoting equal opportunity in employment and education for the community, and it keeps a close eye on legislation related to civil rights of the Chinese. The building that houses CAA was a communications center for Chinese revolutionaries in 1910.

Walter U. Lum. Photo courtesy of Stephanie Ng Kelly,
Mr. Lum's great-great-granddaughter, and family.

Last Days of Yerba Buena

San Francisco was first surveyed in 1839 by civil engineer Jean J. Vioget, who designed a city plaza facing Yerba Buena Cove, where the ships unloaded. He named the streets after historically prominent men. By 1846, there were approximately two hundred people living in Yerba Buena. The small blocks and narrow streets laid out in the original survey are still a part of today's Chinatown.

On July 9, 1846, Captain John Montgomery and seventy-two soldiers and marines came ashore from the *USS Portsmouth* and marched to the Mexican Customs House. A lieutenant read a proclamation prepared by Captain Montgomery claiming the territory for the United States. Accompanied by a twenty-one-gun salute from the *USS Portsmouth*, the troops took down the Mexican flag and raised the Stars and Stripes, and it has flown here ever since. Soon after, a street along the Embarcadero (Spanish for wharf) was named after Captain Montgomery. Once known as the Barbary Coast, Montgomery Street is just one block away from Kearny, and parallel to it.

By the end of July 1846, a young man named Sam Brannan arrived on the *USS Brooklyn*, along with 238 fellow Mormons. Their arrival practically doubled the population of Yerba Buena. Brannan, twenty-six years old and a sharp dresser, quickly became one of the city's most visible citizens. His purpose in coming here was to escape from the religious persecution, and he was supposed to rendezvous with Mormon leader Brigham Young, who stopped off in Salt Lake City instead. After six months at sea, Brannan was not about to set off again, and settled in the village by the bay.

One can reasonably assume that good food influenced Brannan's decision to stay. The 1840s were a legendary time for San Francisco gourmets because oysters could still be harvested off the floor of the San Francisco Bay. A few years into the Gold Rush, the demand for oysters became so great that the oyster beds of the bay were completely exhausted. By then, though, suddenly rich miners had created a demand for other good things to eat. As early as January, 1050 grocers in gold fields were advertising smoked halibut, dried cod, eggs, ham, beef, molasses, coffee, cheese, chocolate, spices, fresh fig, butter crackers and preserved vegetable, fruits, and meats. All those foods came through San Francisco.

What a coincidence! Fresh oysters are served at one of my favorite restaurants, Bacar, at 448 Brannan Street (named after Sam Brannan). On Thursdays and Fridays, I love showing up for happy hour where oysters on the half shell are discounted to $1.00 each. Otherwise, oysters these days cost up to $3.50 each. BACAR's website is www.bacarsf.com.

The Mormons were surprised at the weather here. It was cool and overcast in the summertime, and much of the future city was made up of windy, treeless sand dunes. Yerba Buena officially became San Francisco on January 30, 1847, when Lieutenant Washington A. Bartlett, the appointed *alcalde* (Spanish for mayor) changed its name from Yerba Buena to correspond with the name of the bay.

GOLD!

If you could ask Portsmouth Plaza what its biggest day ever was, it would probably tell you May 12, 1848. That is when Sam Brannan, who started the city's first newspaper, *California Star*, announced the discovery of gold by marching down Montgomery Street to Portsmouth Plaza holding vials of gold dust. He sent one of his reporters out to Sutter's Fort, now the city of Sacramento, to investigate the rumor that people were paying their bills with gold dust. Legend has it that Sam immediately opened well-stocked mining supply stores in San Francisco and Sutter's Fort to cash in on the gold rush. One thing is more certain: Brannan's announcement, along with the May 19 headline "GOLD! GOLD! GOLD!" in rival newspaper, *The Californian*, set off the largest peacetime migration in United States history.

Like adventurous young men throughout the world, many Chinese came to California with the hope of finding riches in its Gold Country. California soon became known in China as *Gum San*, meaning Gold Mountain. Chinese miners were discriminated against in the gold fields, but cherished as chefs. One of those chefs probably created the most famous of Gold Rush dishes—Hangtown Fry—a scramble of eggs, bacon, and oysters. By the time Mark Twain arrived in the 1860s, most boarding houses had a Chinese chef. The Chinese were healthier than most miners, probably because they drank safely boiled water as tea instead of the polluted fresh water of the rivers.

San Francisco was known as *Gum San Dai Fow*, Big City of the Gold Mountain. I cannot help but visualize tens of thousands of Chinese men leaving their wives and families in China to come to America with suitcases filled with their dreams and hopes. Many thought they would find gold streaming down the mountains, and that, with the new riches, they would return to China as wealthy merchants. Oh, but to dream! In this new land, the Chinese men kept their diets familiar and comforting. A typical meal might have been steamed fish, stir-fried green vegetables, and rice. Later, their meal options expanded to include preserved eggs, vegetables, salted fish and shrimp, dried food products such as bean curd skin, mushrooms, and a variety of soups made with bones of pork, chicken, and beef.

There were many other reasons for people to want to leave China besides the quest for gold. A series of disastrous floods and droughts throughout the nation between 1846 and 1850 resulted in widespread famine. Also, 1851 marked the beginning of the Taiping Rebellion, a civil war that lasted thirteen years and cost millions of lives. It was an uprising meant to free the poor from their terrible conditions. The rebellion was finally crushed by the Qing dynasty, with the help of Western nations and their mercenary soldiers. For most of the nineteenth century, the ordinary people in China suffered greatly from foreign competition, invasions, crime, violence, drug addiction, high taxes, outrageous rents, and unemployment. It is estimated that 2.5 million people left China over the last half of the nineteenth century, with about 320,000 going to North America.

Early settlers came from southern China's Guangdong (formerly Canton) Province around the mouth of the Pearl River, an area about the same size as the San Francisco Bay Area. Its provincial capital is Guangzhou, "south gate of China," about one hundred miles northwest of Hong Kong. Because this area is surrounded by high mountains, it has always been isolated from the rest of China. The Imperial Court in Beijing limited early contact with Westerners to this area to prevent the spread of Western influence throughout China. A high percentage of Chinese now living in the United States have roots in Guangdong.

California's Gold Country was a dangerous place during the 1850s. One doctor estimated that one in five miners died within six months after arriving. Easily mined surface deposits were quickly exhausted, and rewards seldom matched the effort and hazard of going underground, digging, and dynamiting. There was much greed and violence, and disease was rampant due to primitive conditions.

During the 1850s and 1860s, about 80 percent of the Chinese in California were in the Gold Country. Even before the Chinese arrived in great numbers, there was much resentment against "foreigners" coming to dig gold. The Chinese quickly learned that it was not a good idea to compete with Euro-Americans for the most promising sites.

In 1852, the legislature imposed the first of many discriminatory taxes directed at the Chinese. Many tax collectors were violent and unscrupulous toward them. Between 1852 and 1870, for example, over half the state's revenue came from foreign miners' taxes. From 1854 to 1872, the testimony of Chinese, African Americans, and Native Americans was not admissible in court against Euro-Americans. Ironically, the Indians usually thought of the Chinese as another tribe, and left them alone. The Chinese managed to survive by mining sites that were abandoned by Euro-Americans or were less promising. They persisted long after most Euro-Americans had given up and abandoned the Gold Country. By 1873, the Chinese had become the largest ethnic group among miners. Some of their mines continued to operate into the 1880s.

Back from the Gold Country

Because of the extreme labor shortage in San Francisco, conditions were more hospitable than they were in the Gold Country. The would-be millionaires who arrived for the Gold Rush did not want to be bogged down with the everyday chores of cooking and laundry. But there were very few women in the young boomtown to take on these domestic chores that were normally assigned to females. The Chinese were willing to do any kind of work and were much in demand as cooks and domestics in San Francisco. They were often paid more than Euro-Americans who held the same positions. There was a Chinese restaurant in San Francisco as early as July 1849. Non-Chinese quickly learned that Chinese food was an excellent value, being both nutritious and flavorful. Chinese restaurants flourished, and to this day are a popular attraction. Celebrating and sharing food is enormously important in the Chinese culture, so the Chinese restaurant trade evolved naturally.

Because famine and overpopulation have plagued our history, we have learned to emphasize the joy of good food. Almost any excuse will do for holding a banquet, and food budgets are often cast to the wind. Also, the American diet itself seemed strange and barbaric to many newly arrived Chinese. Vegetables grown here were hardly recognizable to them. Shipping records show that huge lots of Chinese food products were imported from China early on. My friend Martha Mew's father was one of those attracted by gold. She tells of how amazed her father was to witness slabs of meat that were brought to the table not yet carved. The Chinese cut, slice, or mince all meat before cooking or serving, and would never put a whole turkey or roast on the table.

Then as now, there was a shortage of fresh water in much of California. Laundry service was available at Washer Woman's Lagoon, a body of fresh water at the foot of Russian Hill in what is now the Marina District, west of Chinatown. It cost $8 to get a dozen shirts done. Since an average month's wage was about $12, laundry was a very expensive service for some and an unaffordable luxury for others. One way of dealing with this problem was to wear clothes until they wore out or became so offensive that the wearer and his companions could no longer stand them. To cut expenses, some men sent their dirty laundry by clipper ship to Hawaii or Hong Kong, a roundabout solution that took three to six months to complete. The Chinese were quick to exploit this market. Many were badly in need of employment, as they had been squeezed out of the Gold Country by the foreign miners' tax. Requirements were few, and the investment was minimal: a wash tub, fresh water, washboard, and soap. Location was not an important factor because laundrymen picked up and delivered. Often, two laundrymen shared the same premises, with one operating in the day and the other at night. By 1852, the cost of having laundry done had dropped considerably and the tradition of the Chinese laundry was under way.

There were few diversions available, so eating well became the number one form of entertainment. Because of the sudden wealth of the Gold Rush, lavish foods were coming through San Francisco and the city's reputation as a "foodie" town was stamped in gold. Oysters were both expensive and popular. By 1851, there were approximately five hundred bars for a population of twenty-five thousand people, or one saloon for every fifty inhabitants. One of the most popular of these establishments was located on the site of what is now the Hilton Financial District, across from Portsmouth Plaza. The Jenny Lind Theatre was named after the legendary "Swedish Nightingale" in 1852, despite the fact that Lind never actually came to San Francisco on her American tour with showman Phineas T. Barnum. When the city later bought the property to build a city hall, there was a massive demonstration at Portsmouth Square, protesting the razing of the popular theatre.

Real Buried Treasure

In 2001, an exciting discovery was made a few blocks from the Portsmouth Plaza. The hull of a great nineteenth-century ship was unearthed during excavation for new construction. Built in 1840, the *USS General Harrison* had been deserted by its passengers and crew in 1851. Such was the fate of gold ships, frequently abandoned by crews and captains who merely wanted passage to the California gold fields. They often dumped unwanted cargo into the bay.

Over sixty thousand gold seekers arrived between 1849 and 1850, sometimes on boats so derelict they barely survived the trip. The *USS General Harrison* was eventually buried under what is now the corner of Battery and Clay. This is the former location of the legendary *dim sum* restaurant, Yank Sing, which was torn down to make way for an eleven-story building. *Dim sum* is extremely popular. It is a way of life in the Chinese culinary world and is best compared to today's popular "small plates" or *tapas*, except that most *dim sum* dishes are bite-size pieces of steamed dumplings filled with pork and shrimp, and wrapped in a thin skin made from flour, egg, and water. Yank Sing's appropriately named "gold fish" steamed dumplings are still served at its two other locations, 101 Spear Street and 49 Stevenson Street (www.yanksing.com). The "gold fish" are simply a cute rendition of the traditional shrimp dumpling, but shaped into bite-size "fish" with bits of carrots for eyes and a twist of the wrapper to form a tail.

THE BUDDHIST UNIVERSAL CHURCH and THE CHINESE TELEPHONE EXCHANGE

On the north side of Portsmouth Plaza, across Washington Street, sits the Buddhist Universal Church (720 Washington, at Kearny). The church was built on an infamous historical site from the wild days of the old Barbary Coast strip. One of the first Chinese nightclubs in San Francisco, Wilbur Wong's Club Mandalay, kept revelers happy here through the first half of the twentieth century.

The church's congregation purchased the nightclub in 1951 and incorrectly calculated that a mere $500 would be sufficient to remodel it into a church. As soon as the papers were signed, the city condemned the building because three of its four walls were structurally unsound, and ordered it to be torn down. This created a huge financial problem for the congregation. But after eleven years of volunteers' hard work, they rebuilt the church. When lack of money threatened to stop the construction, members of the congregation volunteered time for baking projects—wrapping and selling cookies. The church's slogan might as well have been: "No cookies, no concrete ... no concrete, no church." Work continued every evening and weekend. Thanks to additional donations and financial assistance from the community, it became known affectionately as the Church of a Thousand Hands.

> In his book, Bridging the Pacific, historian Thomas Chinn reports that architect Worley Wong immersed himself in Buddhist studies before he could begin work on the church plans in 1952. Dr. Paul Fung, leader of the church, described it during dedication ceremonies on March 1, 1963: "The church has a golden colored main chapel inside the entrance, and a hammered bronze wall that shows off Buddha seated under a bodhi tree. On the mezzanine there is another chapel, the Monastery of the Bamboo Grove, modeled after a famous place where Buddha gave lectures 2,500 years ago."

Today, the Buddhist Universal Church is especially busy around the Lunar New Year when a bilingual play is staged for several weeks during the festivities. Other activities include weddings conducted in Chinese and/or English.

The Buddhist Universal Church

United Commercial Bank (the Former Chinese Telephone Exchange)

Kitty-corner from Portsmouth Plaza, walk up Washington Street half a block towards Grant Avenue. Get out your cameras for the second most photographed site in Chinatown—the United Commercial Bank, located at 743 Washington Street. The most photographed site is the Gateway to Chinatown on Grant and Bush. The bank is known by the locals as the former Chinese Telephone Exchange. Wok Wiz tour leader Lola Hom gave me a copy of the original phone book to show to our visitors. Lola's father used it for many years while living in Chinatown. The original building was destroyed in the 1906 earthquake, and in 1909 the current building was constructed. In 1949, the Pacific Telephone and Telegraph Company switched to the dial system, so the telephone exchange went out of business and the building was sold. The former Bank of Canton purchased and restored the building in 1960. In 2004, the United Commercial Bank became the newest occupant of the former Chinese Telephone Exchange building.

United Commercial Bank, the former Chinese Telephone Exchange.

The Chinese Telephone Exchange may have been the only foreign-language telephone exchange in the United States. Over twenty primarily female operators spoke several dialects of Chinese as well as English. They memorized all the phone numbers because most of the customers calling the operator to be connected asked for people by name, and it was a common belief that it was rude to refer to people as numbers. And, because the Chinese lived in such a small area of five blocks, there were few secrets. If you received a phone call at home while you were out visiting family or friends, someone would know how to locate you. If there was a long-distance telephone call, someone would send a little boy or girl to find you. This was old-style "child care." It was common practice for children to go to work with their parents, and, as they grew older, they helped out in all ways possible.

The cover and a page from the old Chinese Telephone Directory, 1942. Phone directory courtesy of Lola Hom.

The old Chinese Telephone Exchange building was once the location of publisher Sam Brannan's *California Star* newspaper office. The two-story building epitomizes Chinese architecture, with its pagoda style; vivid, bright colors of red, green, and a bit of gold; and three distinct roofs with turned up eaves to ward off evil spirits. One clever ten-year-old visitor suggested that evil spirits got "tangled in the eaves so they could not hurt anyone."

Snack Time

Now that you have become acquainted with the Portsmouth Plaza area, it is time to take a break and have a snack or two. One of my favorite places to stop is considered a hole-in-the-wall, but with a clean kitchen. You's Dim Sum (675 Broadway, 415-788-7028) is known for their over-sized baked pork buns, a somewhat sweet bun that is loaded with minced roast pork. Or, order a variety of finger-licking-good steamed dumplings to eat as you stroll along the Chinatown streets.

If you are hungry for more than a snack, cross over to the corner of Stockton and Broadway, to Yuet Lee (1300 Stockton, 415-982-1620). On the outside, you will see a big Coca Cola sign instead of the restaurant name. Intense lucky colors of neon-green and red identify the place, too. In the wee hours of the night, this is a magnet for many of the top chefs from all over San Francisco. It often fills up with the "who's who" of haute cuisine after they close their own kitchens. Before he moved to Chicago to become the executive chef of Bin 36 restaurant, former San Francisco Chef John Caputo and I had a magnificent culinary send-off at Yuet Lee. I hope Chef John and his wife have now discovered my favorite Chinese restaurant in Chicago's Chinatown, Emperor's Choice.

Yuet Lee is known for fresh fish and crab, straight from the tanks. The owners, brothers Tim and Sam, are very obliging in offering suggestions. Sometimes, I bring my "I Can't Believe I Ate My Way Through Chinatown!" group here for an impromptu snack of "salt and pepper calamari" on our way to lunch.

Okay, let's work up another appetite by walking some more to explore new places.

CHAPTER 2
HERBAL MEDICINE

Traditional Chinese medicine is an ancient practice. Herbal medicine has long been a respected practice in China, involving rigorous training and education. By the beginning of the twentieth century, the number of codified prescriptions had grown to 2,500. They were made from pure herbs, just as they are today all over China and wherever large Chinese populations live. Today in China, herbal medicine and Western medicine are taught side by side in medical schools.

As you observe Chinatown residents, you will notice a large number of elderly, healthy-looking Chinese going about their daily business. Most of these Chinese senior citizens attribute their clear eyes and skin to years of consuming Chinese teas and soups composed of various roots, herbs, and bones. They find these items in over thirty active herbal shops in Chinatown. You can spot an herbal shop by its aroma and by the sight of entire walls filled with hundreds of small, wooden drawers (like library card catalogs) containing the herbs. The herbalists who run the shops are often teamed up with doctors of traditional Chinese medicine who have an office in the back.

Peek in an herbal shop, and you may see the herbalist chatting with the patient as he carefully weighs the contents of a prescription on an old balance scale. Combinations from hundreds of roots, herbs, nuts, seeds, and dates constitute remedies for myriad ailments. On our walking tours, we drop in to visit a Chinese herbal medicine shop. An introduction to the herbalist and doctor begins with a friendly nod and "good morning." We point out the many unusual looking items that those of us who grew up in Chinatown take for granted. I still wrinkle up my nose when my mother prescribes a certain foul-tasting tea for a cold. It is fun to watch a group grimace when I suggest they try some tree bark tea or bits of ginseng root.

Like so much of life in Chinatown, these herbal shops have a tradition that reflects the immigrant status of the Chinese in San Francisco. The first Chinese in America had to depend on each other for medical care because they could not speak English, were excluded from white hospitals, and often might not have been able to afford the medical expenses anyway. Entrusting life-and-death decisions to strangers and strange treatments would have caused more anxiety than solace. And all of the religions and philosophies of China taught that anxiety was the enemy of good health. Therefore, most early settlers brought little bags of herbal remedies with them from their homeland.

Though the Chinese were reluctant to venture to Western doctors, some very prominent whites sought treatment from the Chinese. Around the turn of the century, a pharmacist named Li Po Ti established a very successful practice in an alley off Jackson Street. He and his associates treated between 150 and 300 patients a day. He was famous for his cure for rheumatism. Among his patients were half the Big Four—Leland Stanford and Mark Hopkins, the railroad barons who lived on Nob Hill. Li Po Ti earned an estimated $75,000 a year and became one of the biggest landowners in Chinatown.

Preventive Medicine

The Chinese have a different view of medicine than Westerners, who tend to consult a doctor after developing symptoms of illness. The Chinese visit doctors to stay healthy. My parents used to say that seeing a doctor after you become ill is like digging a well after you become thirsty. The Chinese prefer to buy ingredients for herbal teas and soups as preventive medicine, or simply for maintenance of good health, preferring natural healing to pills or shots.

Chinese medicine has philosophical roots in the Taoist principle that all life consists of a delicate balance of the opposing forces of yin and yang. We believe that most diseases are long-term, systemic, and nutrition-based, which explains why the distinction between Chinese pharmacies and food stores has always been blurry.

Because medicine has always been a soft science, dependent on observations and trial-and-error experiments, herbal medicine has necessarily been built upon such tradition. Chinese herbal shops today carry over-the-counter prescriptions for minor ailments; the pharmacist dispenses a prescription after the client describes his or her ailment. From time to time, I prepare chicken herbal soup for my family, not because anyone is feeling ill, but as preventive care. For more serious ailments, a patient consults a physician who will prescribe herbal medicine especially for him. Physicians generally give patients a pulse diagnosis that lasts several minutes. The Chinese doctors have identified at least twelve different pulses, each of which indicates the condition of a vital organ. The doctor has the patient rest his wrist on a pillow while the doctor takes the various pulses with great concentration. A diagnosis also involves looking into the patient's eyes and at his tongue.

In the back room of the herbal shop, the Chinese doctor typically asks the patient questions about his daily life, some of which may seem irrelevant. His purpose is to see if the patient's system needs speeding up or slowing down. Having completed his examination, the doctor determines the internal imbalances of the patient and then writes a prescription for a Chinese pharmacist to follow. Prescriptions consist of an assortment of barks, berries, nuts, roots, dried flowers, and other animal or mineral cures that have been used for centuries. Often, the bill will be tabulated with an abacus—the original computer and the "Chinese cash register."

At home, the prescriptions are brewed for the length of time it takes to brew a strong tea. The usual method is to heat up four rice bowls of water, add the ingredients, and then cook until it is reduced to one rice bowl of liquid. Strain and drink. Like a lot of medicine, the concoction is usually bitter tasting. We eat a small envelope worth of California golden raisins to counteract the bitterness. When I was a little girl, I would eat the raisins first and pour some of the tea down the drain when my parents were not watching. I usually got caught. Now that I am an adult, I thank my parents for making us drink those teas, contributing to my "high energy."

Some prescriptions are meant to be topical, requiring the mixing of sugar with the tea to thicken it before direct application to prescribed parts of the body. Repeat visits to the herbalist are often necessary for further pulse examinations and modifications of the prescription. I have met many people who found relief only at the herbalist.

In the past, herbalists have come under close scrutiny for violating medical laws in the United States. However, the State of California now licenses practitioners of herbal medicine.

Favorite Herbal Shops in Chinatown

Wan Hua Co., 665 Jackson Street (corner of Wentworth Alley). I have known the herbalist, York So, for over twenty-five years, and he looks the same as he always has. Perhaps it is because he practices what he preaches. York owns a very small "mom and pop" herbal shop. It is crammed with all sorts of ingredients for your wellness. A non-English-speaking Chinese doctor sits behind a curtain in the back. After he gives the patient a diagnosis, York fills a prescription and tallies up the cost on an abacus.

Great China Herb Co., 857 Washington Street (corner of Spofford Alley). This is the oldest herbal shop in San Francisco, and perhaps in California. Because it is now operated by the third generation, it is a safe bet that non-Chinese-speaking customers and patients will not feel intimidated. There is a traditional Chinese doctor who gives an instant diagnosis for about $15 or less.

Dung Fong Trading Company, 101 Waverly Place. This is a great herbal shop for non-Chinese-speakers. English is spoken here, and Dennis, one of the shop owners, is very friendly and helpful. In addition to a great variety of Chinese herbs, you can find ginseng, dried mushrooms, dried abalone, and a variety of Chinese teas. Some of my tour leaders and I come here for ginseng teabags. We put the bags into bottled water and sip away. Could that be one of the reasons why we have such good energy on our walking tours?

Tung Shing Trading Co., 734 Jackson Street. This very clean, well-lit herbal shop has an in-residence herbalist, Cham Sing. However, you must be able to speak Cantonese to converse with either Sing or his wife. The shop has huge displays of ginseng root, shark's fin, bird's nest, dried scallops, and other items used in herbal soups, tonics, and for cooking.

Wing On Trading, Inc., 728 Jackson Street. This is a very small herbal shop. My mother likes to buy deer antlers here to make a soup for her arthritis. The herbalist slices them into thin pieces after softening up the antler in a microwave.

Superior Trading Company, 837 Washington Street. This is a well-lit, two-level shop that claims to be the largest house of Oriental herbs and ginseng. In the window display, there are plates filled with various dried roots and herbs, as in most herbal shops, for the curious visitor.

Popular Items in a Chinese Herbal/Dry Food Shop

If you are interested in exploring Chinese herbal shops, I have provided information below about the uses of some of the items you will find:

Abalone, dried Upon first appearance, some dry abalone resembles dark rocks. They must be soaked in warm water for several hours. You usually simmer them for hours prior to slicing them and adding them to soup, or serving them whole at elegant culinary occasions. The abalone is rich in flavor and chewy in texture. Fresh abalone is also very popular for use in soups and stir-fry dishes. Abalone soup is a remedy for high fevers, headaches, and insomnia.

Almonds (and other nuts and seeds) A wide variety of nuts, ranging from Chinese almonds (smaller than American ones, almost heart-shaped,) to fox nuts, walnuts, gingko nuts, and lotus seeds are available in Chinese stores. Rich in protein, nuts and seeds are used in soups and for cooking. Almonds are used to suppress coughs and balance your body's energy. Pine nuts cost a fraction in Chinatown of what they cost in Italian import and grocery stores. A few years ago, there was a woman on our tour who went crazy in the herbal shop, buying a package of each kind of nut and seed. When asked what she was going to do with her purchases, she replied that she'd figure that out when she got home, assuming that everything she bought would be good for her. She was right!

Bean Curd Sticks My daughter Tina and granddaughters Maggie and Stella love the *foo jook* that I add to my homemade *jook*. On every tour that I conduct, someone points out and asks about the unusual-looking hard, yellow sticks. They are made from the rich cream that forms on top of heated soymilk, and they come in flat or stick form. The bean curd sticks stand about twelve to fourteen inches long and must be reconstituted in hot water until they change to a light yellow cream color. Cut them into two-inch pieces and add to soups or other recipes. They are always used in *lo han jai*, a traditional Lunar New Year stew.

Bird's Nest These are produced by swallows that live in huge caves in the East Asian tropics. Mating males and females secrete a gelatinous saliva to make nests. The most sought after nests are called white nests, which are almost completely saliva. Less valuable black nests may contain feathers, grasses, and moss. The nests are harvested and dried and must be washed several times before cooking. Believers of the virtues of the nests pay a fortune for this delicacy in order to have a good complexion and because it is considered nutritious.

Black or White Fungus These popular, dried "wood ears" and "cloud ears" come from the mushroom family. If you enjoy Hot and Sour Soup or *Mushu* pork, you have tasted dried black fungus. The white fungus resembles a dry, yellowish sponge about two inches in diameter, and is used in cooking as well as in a dessert soup. Both black and white fungi are said to promote longevity. Black and white fungi do not have much flavor of their own, much like bean cake, but absorb the flavors from food around them. They add a soft but crunchy texture to hot and cold soups and stir-fry dishes.

Chrysanthemum Bagged leaves of chrysanthemum are used for teas that are often requested in the *dim sum* houses. When you order a pot, lift the lid to look at the pretty flowers floating around. Tea made of dried chrysanthemum is taken to relieve eye infections and is used as an eyewash.

Deer Antlers The antlers are often ground for use in herbal tea and are used to increase strength in different ways. When a friend of mine, for example, developed a severe rash from a food allergy in China, her hosts took her to a doctor who rubbed deer antlers on the affected areas. She was fine the next morning. You will often see the herbalist scraping fur from antlers before cutting them into small pieces; the fur is considered a powerful aphrodisiac. Antlers are exported from Ohio and Minnesota to China.

***Fot Choy* or Black Moss** This hair-like moss is gathered along China's southern coast. It has no eye appeal since it looks like an old, black wig. It is considered an excellent source of fiber. *Fot choy* is used as ingredient in *lo han jai*, the Buddhist vegetarian stew that is commonly served for the Chinese New Year. *Fot choy* means prosperity in Chinese, and that is one reason why *lo han jai* is so popular at traditional Chinese New Year dinners.

Ginger Root, fresh Fresh ginger is found more often in grocery stores, but worth a mention here. Sold as ginger root, it is used along with fresh garlic in hundreds of dishes, including soups, fillings for dumplings, steamed and stir-fried dishes, and even in desserts. Ginger stimulates the circulation and is a good remedy for travel nausea/sickness, coughs, and colds.

Ginseng Roots Ginseng is available in dried form, whole, or in slices. The color varies from light to very dark brown. It is considered an energy-booster that promotes the yin energy, while cleaning out excess yang in our bodies, thus providing balance. Ginseng farms in Wisconsin produce a high-quality product that supplies the United States and is exported to Asia. I enjoy using ginseng roots in cooking, sometimes in steamed chicken or added as an ingredient in chicken soup.

Gingko Nuts I remember helping my mother crack gingko nuts with a hammer. The hard, beige shells look like tiny footballs. Sometimes, I hit the shell too hard and accidentally smashed the small, pale-yellow meat inside. Gingko nuts are a popular remedy for bladder and urinary ailments. They are used primarily in soups and claypot stews. Sometimes, gingko nuts are added to the filling for "sticky rice," wrapped in lotus or bamboo leaves.

Lily Stems These golden needles are pale brown and are three to five inches long. They are dried, unopened flowers of yellow and orange day lilies. Medicinally, they are used for mild pain relief. Lily stems are used most commonly in *mushu* pork, steamed entrees, and as an addition to many stir-fried dishes.

Mushrooms, dried These mushrooms are readily available in Asian food markets throughout the country, and of course, all over Chinatown. They range in price from very affordable to expensive. The price of dried mushrooms depends on the quality. Dried mushrooms must be reconstituted in cold or hot water, and you must remove the stems prior to cooking. For special dinners, use the high-end ones with star-like caps and deeper crevices to hold sauces. The less-expensive mushrooms are minced up for fillings in *dim sum* and/or in soups with several other ingredients.

Red Dates The red dates are imported from China and are used in soups to add sweetness. They're also used in a variety of steamed dishes, such as with chicken and black mushrooms. The little dried jujubes are bright red and are used to counteract the bitterness of many Chinese herbal remedies. They are also good for your vision. The red color is auspicious and brings good fortune.

Rhizoma Polygonati *Wai san* in Guangdonese, or "tongue depressors" as I call them. They are white in color, hard in texture, and shaped like tongue depressors. They nourish the stomach and are used as a remedy for dry cough, fever, and dizziness.

Scallops, dried These little, dried up scallops look like gold nuggets. Like most dried vegetables, the scallops must be soaked in hot water for three to four hours, or overnight in cold water. They are rehydrated, cut into thin slices, and added with black mushroom to fried rice or other dishes.

Shark's Fin Shark's fin has long been one of the most revered and expensive food items for the Chinese. It is usually purchased as pieces of hard, dried, grayish fins. A sideways peek reveals golden tendons, the part that is used for soup. The color of the cooked fin is a golden hue, representing prosperity. This soup is usually served at elaborate Chinese banquets at weddings, anniversaries, or for very special friends. They range in price from $100 to over $300 a pound. But it is worth every penny, a good herbalist will explain, because of the energy and vigor it can provide. Unfortunately, the trade in shark's fin is causing a grave problem because it encourages over-fishing that endangers the shark population. Some environmentalists advocate a ban on fishing for shark's fin.

Thousand-Year-Old Eggs I like to order *Pay Donn Sow Gee Yuk Jook*—Chinese Rice Congee with Thousand-Year-Old Eggs and Lean Pork. These eggs are quite a conversation piece. They are duck or chicken eggs, preserved for several months in a mixture of salt, lime, ash, clay, and other ingredients. The yolk turns a dark green, is creamy, and tastes a bit like cheese or mushroom. The egg white turns brown and is almost transparent; it is gelatinous and tasteless.

Tiger Balm This is the brand name of a popular ointment that has been commercially available from Hong Kong for over a half a century. It provides temporary relief for joint pains and muscle soreness, pain from colds, flu, strains, rheumatism, or simple backaches. In China, it is also daubed on the acupuncture points, to relieve headaches for example. A preferred kind from China is "Essential Balm."

White Flower Oil This analgesic balm is available in small to medium-size bottles. Dab a little gently on your temples or under your nose when you are not feeling well. It is used for temporary relief of minor muscular aches and pains due to fatigue, strains, and arthritis. It can also be applied to acupuncture points.

Herbalist York So, of Wan Hua Co., filling a prescription.

CHAPTER 3
GRANT AVENUE

Grant Avenue is the main street of Chinatown and the oldest street in our city. Hispanic settlers called it *Calle de la Fundacion*, Foundation Street. When the Americans took over, the name was changed to Dupont Street, for an officer on the *USS Portsmouth*. After the earthquake in 1906, the name of the street was again changed to Grant Avenue in honor of Civil War general and President Ulysses S. Grant. Some older Chinese still call it "Dupont *Gai*" (*gai* means "street" in Chinese). It's easier for them to pronounce as there is no sound equivalent to "r" in the language of Guangdong. Today, Grant Avenue is filled with shops and restaurants; it's the most popular street for tourists looking for souvenirs.

The Gateway to Chinatown

The Gateway to Chinatown is located at Bush and Grant. You will see two large, carved "*foo* dogs," one on each side of an arched gateway. The fierce-looking dogs protect all who enter and welcome visitors. Each year, thousands of visitors walk through the gate to begin their visit to the most historical neighborhood in San Francisco, the heart of Chinatown.

A friend, T. Kevin Casey, contributes this story about how his father, Tom Casey, an Irish immigrant, helped to build San Francisco's Gateway to Chinatown:

"In December 1969, the merchants of San Francisco's Chinatown had finally gotten approval from the city to build a Gateway to Chinatown. The Moreo Construction Company had won the contract to construct it at Chinatown's southern entrance.

"Walter Moreo, a local contractor of French heritage, had received contract approval from the city, possibly due to the encouragement of his Chinese-born wife. But Walter had a problem. Two of his project managers had already resigned from the job, declaring it unbuildable. Then late on a Friday, Walter was in the middle of trying to convince his last project manager to stay on the project. This gentleman had declared he was tired of dealing with overbearing city officials who wouldn't allow his trucks to block more than one lane.

Besides that, the sloping elevations would not allow the gateway to be level as it had been designed.

"Thomas J. Casey, who had immigrated to San Francisco from his native Ireland fifteen years earlier, stopped by Walter's office to turn in his keys after finishing two other government projects for Moreo. Tom figured he was just picking up his final paycheck when Walter said, 'Hey Tom, come in on Monday. I may have another job for you.' So, on Monday morning, Walter slid the gateway architectural blueprints across his desk. Tom glanced at the plans and said, 'Are you crazy? Your project managers told me this job was unbuildable and I'm just a carpenter.' Walter replied, 'Yes, my third and last project manager just walked off the job Friday night. But you did such a great job getting the last two government projects completed that I know if anyone can figure this out, it's you.'

"Tom took the plans and headed out to the intersection of Grant and Bush. In the pouring rain, he began taking measurements of the elevations and quickly saw what all the project managers and city engineers couldn't: the elevations in the architectural drawing were workable, but everyone had been basing their elevations on the current street levels. It turned out that the Bush Street intersection was higher than it was supposed to be. This improper elevation was due to misplaced underground concrete utility vaults. Tom proposed to the city that the San Francisco Water Department, Pacific Gas & Electric, and Pacific Telephone all be required to dig up Bush Street and lower their vaults by eighteen inches. Tom determined that once they relocated the Bush Street vaults, the entrance on Grant Avenue could be built and traffic could handle the grade changes between the down-sloping Bush Street and the up-sloping Grant Avenue.

"The city accepted Tom's recommendation that the three local utilities relocate their vaults, and Tom was able to take advantage of Bush Street's extra lane closures while the utility companies ripped up the intersection at Grant Avenue. But as soon as construction began, he had a run-in with one overly aggressive meter maid who kept climbing around barricades to give the construction trucks tickets for parking in a construction zone.

"A week after Tom started building, Mr. O'Connell, the city inspector, had confidence that things were going just fine. He pulled all his men from the site, allowing Tom to work without excessive bureaucratic scrutiny. They even got the meter maid to give them a break.

"There were numerous financial, physical, and bureaucratic challenges along the way. Midway during the relocation of the utility lines and vaults, the intersection and the first block of Grant Avenue had to be quickly paved over so the 1970 Chinese New Year's Parade could maintain its tradition of marching up

Bush Street and turning left onto Grant Avenue. The morning after the parade, a work crew was back ripping out the freshly poured, temporary concrete.

"The final step of the building, or at least what Tom thought was the final step, was hanging up the sign on the entrance. It is inscribed with the saying "*All under heaven is for the good of the people*" by Dr. Sun Yat-sen. In fact, the entire gateway is supposed to allow good spirits to pass, but to block evil spirits. Unfortunately, as Tom hung the sign and started to dust it off, a local merchant came running up across Bush Street screaming in Cantonese and waving his hands. He communicated that something was reversed and would end up keeping evil spirits in Chinatown. Sure enough, a woman in high heels went around the construction barricade and literally walked ankle-deep into the freshly poured concrete walkway. Needless to say, the sign was quickly turned right side up and hopefully pedestrians no longer trip walking through the Gate."

Old St. Mary's Church

Old St. Mary's Church is a towering and beautiful presence on the northeast corner of the intersection of Grant and California. It is a welcome sight as you walk into Chinatown after taking some pictures at the Gateway.

The Church, originally called St. Mary's Church, was built in 1854 and was established by Father Henry Ignatius Stark. Chinese laborers built the church, which was destroyed in the 1906 earthquake, only to be rebuilt in 1909. Parts of the Church were built with granite imported from China.

Let's Go Shopping

Use all your senses in Chinatown, and have your camera ready. Look at the neon signs, the ornate, towering buildings with curved roofs, the bright colors; listen to the singsong sounds of the nearby cable cars, of the Chinese speaking in their native tongues; smell the earthy aromas of dried foods, Chinese herbs, and mouth-watering cooked food. You are being transported to another country, and you do not need to buy an airline ticket. You are in "Hong Kong by the Bay."

Chinatown's main thoroughfare extends eight blocks, from Bush and Grant Avenue to Broadway. There is much to see on this famous street, but do not miss the side-street extensions to the west and east. It is easy to spend several hours exploring here. Take your time to find the best deals. The two blocks from Bush to California have upscale antique shops, furniture stores, art goods, and silks. Many of the Grant Avenue businesses are not just for tourists. They cater to the everyday needs of locals, with dry goods shops, herbal shops, grocery stores, beauty salons, stationery shops, laundries, banks, restaurants, and family and district associations.

Some of my favorite stores are on Grant Avenue, but many more are located on the side streets. Chinatown is like an octopus, with Grant Avenue in the middle and tentacles going every which way. Chinese residents go about their daily lives in this vibrant, living community. You are a guest here, so do take your time and enjoy our neighborhood.

Anxious Wok Wiz guests—"Did you say shopping bargains on Grant Avenue?"

Some people like to take breaks between meals. Grant Avenue provides most of the mainstream shopping options available in Chinatown. Grant Avenue IS Chinatown. If you enter from the main gate on the south end of Chinatown, here are some of the shops that can entertain you until you get hungry again. Along the way, we will make a stop at the Red Blossom Tea Company where we will get a quick lesson and sample some wonderful tea.

Tai Nam Yang Furniture Co., 438 Grant Avenue. I could not resist buying an adorable ceramic frog standing on its hind legs, holding a box. In the box, I put Chinese "lucky candy" for our guests. The store carries solid rosewood, ebony wood, and other Oriental furniture, lamps, and accessories. It is filled with great gift ideas, such as the raku-fired Nambu teapots that art museum gift stores sell at considerably higher prices.

China Gem Co., 500 Grant Avenue. Owned by Henry Bong since 1970, China Gem is the kind of shop I like because it is established with a great reputation. It is clean, and the owner is often present. Fine jewelry, ivory, and art are available here.

A "no name" (it truly does not have a name) store at 512 Grant Avenue. The owners are always friendly, and their small store offers the typical souvenirs of San Francisco: sweatshirts, T-shirts, and trinkets.

Imperial Fashion, 564 Grant Avenue. This thirty-year-old store is bright and clean, and features high-quality linen tablecloths, doilies, and pillowcases at excellent prices.

Far East Cafe, 631 Grant Avenue. In business since 1920, this is the only authentic Chinese restaurant left in San Francisco with private dining booths. It was remodeled in 1999 and transports your soul to Hong Kong as you dine on fine Chinese food. In most restaurants, you have to order duck well in advance; the Far East Café, on the other hand, has it available daily. The Far East Cafe roasts all its ducks, pigs, and pork on the premise.

China Bazaar, 667 Grant Avenue. This sprawling store is a fun place for kids to shop. The mezzanine level has wonderful gifts and toys and all sorts of souvenirs.

Chinatown Kites, 717 Grant Avenue. The name says it all. The Chinese are the world's connoisseur kite makers and these are the real thing. Bring children of all ages here. Take the kites and fly them high above the Marina greens.

The Wok Shop, 718 Grant Avenue. I love being in this happy store with owner Tane Chan who greets everyone. If you have a question about woks or cooking, she or one of her friendly staff members will gladly help you. You will find whatever you need for cooking at The Wok Shop, including woks, cleavers, steamers, rice cookers, chinaware, and cookbooks. Web site: www.wokshop.com.

Eastern Bakery, 720 Grant Avenue. This old-time coffee shop is popular with locals, although everyone is welcome. Stop in for a Chinese version of Rice Crispy treats, fried *won ton* bowties, a variety of pastries and buns, or cakes and pies. The bakery is known for its moon cakes, most popular during our annual

Moon Festival celebration. Their claim to fame is that President Bill Clinton dropped in once during a San Francisco visit.

Far East Flea Market, 729 Grant Avenue. This gigantic emporium has been in operation since 1984. You can find bargains here, as expected in a flea market. Pause at the intersection of Grant and Commercial for a look down the hill at the San Francisco Ferry Building.

Grant Avenue, the main street in Chinatown.

Kum Tai Jewelry, 811 Clay Street. When my daughter, Tina, was about to get married in July 2001, my mother and I took her here to buy special jewelry for her wedding day. Three friendly brothers have owned and operated the store since 1969. The gold, jade, and pearl necklaces, bracelets, and rings are beautiful, and the prices are fair. I once found a perfect gold fortune-cookie pendant here, and recently, an eighteen-carat gold wok pendant turned into a necklace. Before going back on Grant, walk down to Sing Sang Jewelry at 768 Clay Street if you wish to customize your name in Chinese on a gold necklace.

Asian Image, 800 Grant Avenue. This two-floor store is a welcome addition to Chinatown. The window display is always classy and attractive. Asian Image sells bamboo plants, books on Chinese culture, art, *feng shui*, and beautiful Chinese clothing on the lower level. Web site: www.asianimagesf.com

Red Blossom Tea Company, 831 Grant Avenue. Now we have arrived at Red Blossom Tea Company. Let's go in and meet the sister and brother team of Alice and Peter Luong, tea experts without attitude. Alice is a former investment banker who worked in Hong Kong, and Peter worked in the dot-com industry for several years. Their parents have owned the tea shop for more than twenty years, and now Alice and Peter have "come home" to become its managers. They are friendly and articulate, very bright, accommodating, and a joy to listen to as they talk tea. The shop offers premium teas and artisan tea ware from the Asian continent and other places around the world. We drop in for a quick lesson and tasting of tea, and leave with a greater appreciation of tea drinking. For those who want more, the Luongs welcome you to return for a private tea focus experience. Web site: www.redblossom.com. Phone: (415) 395-0868.

Let us proceed with our tour. Some of the shops we will see on our way to Jackson Street are described below.

Chong Kee Jan, 838 Grant Avenue. This store is located downstairs in the China Trade Center. I have been shopping in this store for more than twenty-five years. It still looks the same. They sell woks, cleavers, pots, claypots, fry pans, steamers, Chinese plates and bowls, chopsticks, books, candy, and souvenirs. You name it, they pretty much have it.

Bow Hon Restaurant, 850 Grant Avenue. Are you hungry? My Wok Wiz team and I love this place for its *yue sonn*, a traditional Lunar New Year raw fish dish. But you might prefer a plate of *chow mein*, or a piping hot "claypot," which is their specialty.

Suey Chong, 900 Grant Avenue. This is a great stop for teachers looking for books for children and other Chinese-related material for their classes.

Merchant of China, 930 Grant Avenue. This is one of the few stores on Grant that still offers silk brocade fabric. They have excellent quality gift items, beautiful Pashmina scarves, lovely jade, pearls, high-quality linens, antiques, the popular Nambu teapots, and beautiful clothing, such as silk tops, pajamas, and kimonos. This is my favorite store for offbeat purses and tote bags. The jade, pearls, and sparkling jewelry are great buys. Say hello to managers Celine and Maxine.

Ginn Wall Hardware, 1016 Grant Avenue. The oldest Chinatown hardware store is still operated by the Der brothers. Ginn Wall is another "must stop" for anyone who likes to cook. From cookbooks and cleavers to moon cake presses, woks, utensils, rice cookers, and vegetable shredders, this store is filled with everything I want for my kitchen, and more. They also sell industrial-size woks to restaurants.

Golden Gate Bakery, 1029 Grant Avenue. You know this place must be popular because long lines form early every morning. The fresh custard tarts, almond cookies, and homemade pastries have gained quite a following.

Mayerson's, 1101 Grant Avenue. Mayerson's is my favorite place to introduce fresh Chinese vegetables such as Chinese swamp spinach, matrimony vine, lotus root, bitter melon, fuzzy squash, winter melon, and fruits such as durian and lychee, all of which are displayed on the street. Inside, check out the fine meat and poultry, fresh and trimmed. You will also find more fruits, several varieties of tofu, yellow and green chives, shallots, soy milk, and dumpling wrappers.

Yee's Restaurant, 1131 Grant Avenue. This is one of my favorite stops for roast duck, salt and pepper crab, and whole steamed fish. Yee's prepares roast and pressed ducks, whole steamed chickens, whole roasted pigs, steamed-to-bright-orange cuttlefish, and soy sauce squabs. Peek inside the window and you will see one of the workers chopping off a slab of roast suckling pig for a customer. Regulars know what time to show up for the freshest pork and for "happy hour" bargain prices: sometime between the lunch and dinner rush. The clientele is 90 percent Chinese, which means the locals enjoy dining here—and that is as reliable an index for travel dining as there is, right?

Ming Kee Game Birds (1136 Grant Avenue), **On Sang Poultry** (1114 Grant Avenue), **Man Sung Market** (1116 Grant Avenue). These three markets sell chickens, quail, chicken feet, fish, and meat. Visitors seem to enjoy walking by to look and make faces at unfamiliar items, such as the "silky chicken," which is black in color. The On Sang Poultry market sells freshly killed chickens, while Ming Kee sells the live chickens for customers to take home.

Chinese menus hang on the walls and contain some yummy dishes that will not be on the English-language menus. Check out what diners are eating, and if it looks tantalizing, tell the server that is what you want.

Tempting Chinese food for in-restaurant dining or for take-out at Yee's Restaurant on Grant Avenue.

CHAPTER 4
JACKSON STREET

At the corner of Grant and Jackson, a detour east (downhill to your right) takes you to one of the great restaurant blocks of Chinatown. This is one of my favorite streets for taking pictures. With an eye on traffic, stand in the middle of the street, and you can take a beautiful shot of the many restaurants and businesses that line both sides of the street. Aim your camera further on Jackson, and snap a picture of the San Francisco-Oakland Bay Bridge in all its glory. The Golden Gate Bridge receives a great deal of attention, but I think the Bay Bridge is gorgeous. Of course, that bridge takes me back to my hometown, Oakland.

While strolling around Jackson Street in Chinatown, it is impossible to avoid the food aromas from the restaurants, cafes, *dim sum* joints, and markets. It is fun to peek into windows and go into the Chinese bakeries and take-out restaurants. Flash a smile, look over the food display, and choose an item or three that excite you.

James and Lily Yuan's **Hunan Home**, 622 Jackson Street, is my favorite restaurant on Jackson Street. The friendly couple loves to greet their customers with a smiling "Welcome *home*." Try the Fresh Sizzling Eel or Oysters, or choose from a variety of lunch plates. On weekends, they offer delicious Shanghai *dim sum*.

While most of the *dim sum* menu is Cantonese in origin, Shanghai's style of northern *dim sum* is not too different. Some people say that Shanghai *dim sum* is more refined. I love *siu loong bow*, a traditional Shanghai-style steamed dumpling that contains a sumptuous broth. To eat it, place the dumpling on a Chinese soup spoon, add a little bit of red vinegar and julienned ginger. Take a little bite to release the broth. Suck it up and then eat the dumpling.

Points of Interest

The Great Star Theatre, 636 Jackson Street. It is the San Francisco host for the Chinese Opera troupes. Tickets are often available at the box office, except for opening night.

Heng Loong Foreign Exchange Ltd., 626 Jackson Street. This is a good place to change money and to send or receive money grams to or from all parts of the world.

Star Lunch Diner, 605 Jackson Street. One of the idiosyncratic lunch spots in Chinatown, the old-fashioned lunch counter is usually packed with customers waiting for the Shanghai-style plate lunches amidst the aroma of the "stinky bean curd."

Ng Hing Kee, 648 Jackson Street. All newspapers and periodicals sold here are in Chinese.

Dick Lee Pastry Shop, 716 Jackson Street. It is a tiny cafe with a huge take-out business. During the summer, they also offer a bargain basement, eat-all-you-want *dim sum* special. You see many locals here, always the telltale sign of good quality.

Yung Kee Rice Noodle Co., 732 Jackson Street. It is just across the street from Dick Lee. Lines form early at Yung Kee for fresh *dim sum*. As you enter, you see a wall of pink take-out boxes, ready to be filled with steamed dumplings, pork buns, rice noodles, rice cakes, and other delicacies. Yung Kee is well known and always busy. Wise shoppers go early.

The Chinese Hospital

The Chinese Hospital (located at 835 Jackson Street) is currently the only independently owned hospital in San Francisco dedicated to a specific cultural group, offering health care services for the Chinese community. In 1900, the Tung Wah Dispensary opened in Chinatown to provide Western and Eastern medical care for the Chinese who were denied access to other healthcare institutions in San Francisco. By 1923, fifteen community organizations had created the Chinese Hospital Association, a nonprofit corporation that raised funds to build the hospital. In 1975, an addition right next door to the Chinese Hospital was greatly welcomed to the community. Today, the Chinese Hospital has approximately 235 physicians, including a wide range of specialists. Although the hospital is in Chinatown, its patient population comes from all over San Francisco and the surrounding area. Still, according to Vice Chief of Staff Dr. Fred Hom, "There is no other hospital in the country where 99 percent of the patients are Chinese or of Chinese origin."

Jackson Street photographed from Grant Avenue, aimed towards Kearny. See the San Francisco-Oakland Bay Bridge in the background.

CHAPTER 5
STOCKTON STREET

Chinatown's Marketplace

We're going to climb a steep hill now and visit that part of Chinatown where most tourists never venture, but where true food-hearts find the dumpling, the fish, and the custard apple of their eye. We're going to Stockton Street, the open-air food market in Chinatown.

There are food markets everywhere you look on Stockton Street. On our tours, we walk through several of the open markets, mostly to observe and introduce vegetables and other food items that may be new to our visitors' eyes. Since many Chinatown residents own only a small refrigerator or none at all, they shop daily. Additionally, the food is so fresh, it makes sense to make a daily sojourn here or to eat out often.

Stockton Street is one block uphill and parallel to Grant Avenue. Locals shop mainly for food here. Visitors interested in Chinese cooking love to explore the bustling markets and shops. I often see chef friends shopping for fresh fish, vegetables, noodles, and other food staples for their restaurants. The number 30 bus, dubbed "the Orient Express," transports you here from Union Square or Fisherman's Wharf. One block west (uphill) of Stockton Street is Powell, where you can hop on a cable car (look for the brown cable car stop signs). Stockton Street's bargain clothing and dry goods stores give way to the real business of this thoroughfare—food. The street is so alive and colorful. Delivery trucks are constantly coming and going with fresh, dancing fish and other seafood. You will see brilliant greens and oranges, representing many types of Chinese vegetables, as well as fruits galore.

Dim sum restaurants and coffee shops bunch together on Stockton, north of Clay. **Little Paris** (939 Stockton), **Fortune Star Cafe** (930 Stockton), **San Sun** (941 Stockton), and the **Joy Hing BBQ Noodle Shop** next door all have their loyal followings. On Stockton Street, north of Jackson, there are more *dim sum* cafes, bakeries, and teahouses.

Many busy San Franciscans find it easy to drop by Chinatown after work to pick up dinner on the way home. It is fun to look through the windows of the many Chinese delicatessens that display cooked Chinese food. Some types of food appear very tempting, while others may appear too exotic for the non-Chinese. Chinese roast pork, whole roast duck, and chickens cooked in soy sauce or steamed hang above trays of duck and chicken feet. Broccoli beef shares a front window with vegetarian stew, *chow mein*, fried rice, fermented black bean, stuffed bitter melon, and braised pig intestines or octopus. Whole roast suckling pigs with crackling skin hang in many shops and may be purchased by the pound. The restaurants usually charge for food by the pint, and the prices are quite reasonable. If you purchase a duck, chicken, or roast pork, it will be chopped up for you, unless you ask otherwise. I always announce, "No head, neck, or tail," before the chef raises his cleaver. You may wish to do the same. Many of the delicatessens are located inside a restaurant, providing a choice of eating in or taking the food out.

Stockton Street is always filled with busy shoppers.

The great supermarkets of Chinatown are further north on Stockton Street. On the east side of the street, several flow onto the sidewalk, offering the most tempting of exotic fruits. I once counted six different varieties of mangos and four different kinds of papayas in one store. You may also find durians from Asia. These are shipped frozen to cut their strong and often offensive aroma. They are known as "the limburger cheese of the fruit world," having a taste that is appreciated, even craved, but only by gourmets able to get beyond the durian's unpleasant smell. Lychees, rambutans, pomelos, custard apples, cherimoyas, coconuts, and red bananas are as common here as avocados, cherries, strawberries, pineapples, and oranges. Inside these stores, thousand-year-old eggs and preserved duck eggs, contained in large ceramic pots, are delicacies worth pursuing.

There are mom-and-pop stores as well as supermarkets—too many to name—all along Grant Avenue, Stockton Street, Jackson, Clay, and Broadway. Everything you need for Chinese cooking is available: soy and oyster sauces, dried mushrooms of various grades and prices, tea, condiments, rice wines, dried noodles, bean curd sticks, and fresh wrappers for *won ton*, *dim sum*, egg rolls, and pot stickers.

Travelers shopping for oils and sauces should avoid breakable glass containers. If you do purchase anything in glass containers, put it into a sealable plastic bag and wrap it in towels to avoid breakage. If you want to avoid packing and carrying purchases with you, ask store managers if they ship goods.

On weekends, this street can seem as crowded as a Hong Kong ferryboat, so those who feel uneasy with crowds might consider saving this area for a weekday visit. On the west side of Stockton, three adjacent stores offer some of California's freshest and most exotic fish and seafood:

New Sang Sang, at 1147 Stockton Street, is filled with live fish tanks. **Pacific Seafood**, at 1143 Stockton Street, is a dried seafood purveyor. **Luen Fat Market**, 1135 Stockton Street, has fish so fresh that some jump out of their boxes onto the sidewalk.

Further north on Stockton, the border of Chinatown and North Beach blurs as Chinatown has overflowed into the old Italian neighborhood of North Beach. There are several inexpensive hotels on or near Stockton Street: The Florence, Castro, Sestri, and Tang Fat.

East Wind Books and Arts, 1435 Stockton Street, is a small, but mighty bookstore that offers a great variety of books on Chinese/Asian history, food, culture, and, of course, the arts.

North of Broadway, you will find the **Mee Mee Bakery** at 1328 Stockton Street. Simon Chow's bakery is popular for its mooncakes, with exotic versions drawing long lines of customers. The traditional mooncakes have gone trendy—they vary with the seasons. Try the honeydew or green tea mooncakes. Mee Mee makes and sells fortune and almond cookies as well.

Little Garden Seafood Restaurant is up the hill at 750 Vallejo, next to the Central Police Station. Most diners order by pointing to a special menu on the wall, written in Chinese, or hope a friendly server will be a translator.

CHAPTER 6
ROSS ALLEY

Seeing all this food has probably made you hungry again, but before we stop for a snack, would you like to meet a local celebrity? We'll find him in Ross Alley.

Ross Alley is narrow but full of life.

My favorite alley, Ross Alley, is located between Sacramento and Washington, and Grant and Stockton. My good friend John Louie moved his fresh **Wo Chong** tofu shop from Jackson Street to this narrow yet busy alley. On a sunny day, look up and you will see laundry hanging out of dozens of windows; the clothes that are air-drying seem to be waving down to you. This is testimony that many families still reside in small apartments throughout Chinatown and may not have access to washers and dryers. They revert to the good old way of sun-drying clothes.

In the middle of Ross Alley, you can sometimes hear children practicing martial arts at the Yau Kung Moon kung fu studio. The Yau Kung Moon lion dance team is very popular, especially during Chinese holidays, festivals, and, of course, the Lunar New Year parade. It is at the Yau Kung Moon studio where students learn about Chinese tradition, culture, discipline, and responsibility, while exercising at the same time. The **Golden Gate Fortune Cookie Factory** is nearby at 56 Ross Alley. Next door, Jun the barber announces "One dollar, one minute" for haircuts. Jun is a celebrity these days, having a bit role in the 2007 movie, *In Pursuit of Happyness*, starring Will Smith. Jun sits on a stool outside of his shop and plays his violin, or the beautiful Chinese instrument, the Chinese fiddle, called an *er-hu*. When we walk along Ross Alley and see Jun, he will grab his *er-hu* and entertain our guests, leaving them with happy hearts and smiles as he rushes back in to continue cutting hair.

Farther down on Ross near Washington Street, there is a colorful wall mural that depicts daily life in Chinatown. The mural scenes include a man carrying a sack of rice over his shoulder and a young lady holding a pink bag filled with oranges and a deeper pink box full of *dim sum*.

Jun, the er-hu playing barber.

CHAPTER 7
SPOFFORD ALLEY

After our walk through Ross Alley, let's walk by Spofford—another signifi-cant alley. Spofford Alley is parallel to Grant and Stockton, and intersected by Washington and Clay. Once housing opium dens, *mah jong* parlors, and broth-els, Spofford Alley was the location of the Chinese Free Masons, at number 36. Here, Dr. Sun Yat-sen, founder of the Chinese Republic, met with the Chinese Freemasons to discuss his dreams for China. He published the *Chinese Free Press*.

Dorothy Quock, Wok Wiz tour leader, was born at 35 Spofford Alley on the second floor in apartment 18. She describes it as, "Two small rooms for our family of eight in typical, tenement-type housing. Usually a community kitchen was at one end of the hallway, and bathroom facilities at the other end. These common areas were shared by everyone on that floor. For illiterate, poor immi-grant women like my mother, home births were not unusual in the 1930s."

In my discussion with Dorothy Quock, I learned that the Chinese Freemasons was a somewhat secret society incorporated in 1879 as a fraternal order. It was formed for mutual aid, protection, and socializing. However, the Masons got involved with illegal activities and had connections with the Chinese all over the world. This served the purposes of Dr. Sun Zhong-shan (Sun Yat-sen), who is considered the George Washington of China, when he was seeking support. He was incognito in Chinatown at least six times.

Dr. Sun Zhong-shan came over to the Chinese Freemasons often between 1896 and 1911. He used their newspaper to advocate political reform and suc-ceeded in forming a revolutionary network. Rumors were that he received over eleven million dollars from the Chinese Freemasons and succeeded in overthrowing the Qing Dynasty. Dr. Sun Zhong-shan was chosen as the first president of the Republic of China in 1912. He had the power to legitimize the Chinese Freemasons. You can still see the three-story building with the red facade that served as the headquarters of the Masons. However, it is no longer such a political meeting place, but more a social meeting place. Today, as in most alleys, you can hear the clicking sounds of *ma-jong*, the popular tile game played throughout Chinatown.

CHAPTER 8
COMMERCIAL STREET

The aroma of dried shark's fin, dried scallops, and dried mushrooms tell me I'm back in what was my neck of the woods for ten years. There are still a couple of shops that sell preserved fish, preserved Chinese sausages, and other dried foods for Chinese cooking. You can stop here for a little lunch, either at **City View** (662 Commercial), or for a rice plate or simple noodle dishes across the street at the **New Hong Kong Menu** restaurant (667 Commercial) that is packed with lunch crowds.

From 1996 to 2006, Wok Wiz's office was at 654 Commercial Street, located off of Kearny, between Sacramento and Clay. My friend Alberta Chinn, who grew up playing on Commercial Street, tells me, "Most of my memories of Commercial Street are from when I was five years old to about eleven. My aunt owned a sewing factory, producing jeans for Levi Strauss. I made friends all over Commercial and remember getting free labels from McCoy Label Company, now the Pacific Heritage Museum." I asked what she did with the labels, because she was so happy to tell this story. "Oh, I played with them, much like what children do today with stickers!" She also got free paper from the Lambrose Paper Company, on the corner of Montgomery and Commercial. She laughs when she adds, "I got free Green River drinks, too. It is a mixture of syrup and 7-Up soda." Alberta must have been quite a charmer to receive so many free treats. She also recalls being scolded by a couple, who used to live at what is now my office, for running up and down Commercial, screaming at the top of her lungs for no apparent reason. No wonder she has such a good command of her voice when she tells her tales.

Wok Wiz tour leader Lola Hom has memories of living on Commercial Street with her family. She recalls, "I was four years old, and I remember standing on the enclosed balcony by myself to watch the Lunar New Year parade on Grant Avenue." Lola also remembers several shrimp processing shops and a Chinese sausage factory on Commercial and Grant.

Today, 654 Commercial Street is home to a gifted couture designer, Victor Tung. This very talented and friendly designer can take one of your favorite dresses or outfits and give it a new life. It is a delight to walk by my old office and see a different ensemble on the mannequin each day. Good luck, Victor!

Pacific Heritage Museum

A few doors from my former office, the Pacific Heritage Museum at 608 Commercial is located on the site of the original San Francisco Mint, which was built in 1854. Visitors can look at the vaults and a historical display about the building. The museum features changing exhibitions on economic and cultural exchanges across the Pacific. It is open Monday through Friday from 11:00 AM to 4:00 PM, and admission is free.

Wells Fargo History Room

Around the corner from the Pacific Heritage Museum is the Wells Fargo History Room (420 Montgomery). The display cases here tell the Gold Rush story and Wells Fargo's contribution to it. This museum is open from 9:00 AM to 5:00 PM, Monday through Friday.

CHAPTER 9
FAMILY AND DISTRICT ASSOCIATIONS

Let's move along now to a side street that served as the support system for several generations of new Chinese immigrants in San Francisco.

The homes of family and district associations along Waverly Place are some of Chinatown's most visually impressive buildings. Casual visitors sometimes incorrectly assume that they are savings and loan institutions. In early Chinatown, family representatives and interpreters met new arrivals and provided food, lodging, and employment. As the name implies, family associations include all people who have a common surname and relatives remotely related by blood or marriage. The family associations expanded to become "kinship associations," with members from different, but usually nearby villages and districts. The associations provided the only form of social control within the Chinese community. Many of the associations have headquarters on Waverly Place. The nearby home of Six Companies, the Chinese Consolidated Benevolent Association, is at 843 Stockton Street.

I belong to the Kwong, Louie & Fong Association, on the corner of Grant and Clay. The view from our balcony is stunning. When I first became a member of this association, I stood on the balcony and quietly thanked my ancestors for their contribution to San Francisco's Chinatown.

*The Kwong, Louie & Fong Association, also known as the Soo Yuen Benevolent
Association, 806 Clay (and Grant)*

Because San Francisco was the central point of entry for Chinese into the United States, associations gained great power over all Chinese in the United States and played a role in resolving outstanding debts for those who returned to China. This was no coincidence because the associations often provided passage for the debtors' journey to America under the credit ticket system, levying a fee up to twenty dollars to issue an exit permit to those who left America. The steamship lines agreed not to sell tickets to anyone who did not have an exit permit. Associations had representatives at the docks to collect the permits from departing Chinese. This arrangement between the associations and steamship lines continued well into the twentieth century.

In 1851, the first district associations, then known as meeting halls, formed in San Francisco. District associations have existed in China for hundreds of years. They originally consisted of groups of traveling merchants and craftsmen who joined to promote their economic interests and to provide charitable and social benefits to the members. Because Chinese society was so closed and immobile, considerable differences in the dialects and customs existed, even in an area as small as Guangdong province. People with a common heritage associated with one another. The most literate and affluent merchants in the community generally controlled these associations. Family associations made up power blocs within the district associations. Merchants and elders, who had their family honor at stake, administered the associations.

The family and district associations fragmented and expanded rapidly between the Gold Rush and the Exclusion Act of 1882. Early in the 1850s, a committee of association presidents formed to represent the community at large. Its purpose was to peacefully resolve disputes among associations, to entertain political dignitaries from China, and to represent the business and political interest of Chinatown to the outside world. This committee evolved over the next two decades to become The Chinese Consolidated Benevolent Association, or Six Companies.

The Six Companies was officially founded on November 19, 1882, and incorporated under the laws of California in 1901. The Six Companies operated much like a court of appeals, resolving disputes between businesses and associations. It served as a witness to the signing of contracts between businesses. Its attorneys vigorously fought discriminatory laws in San Francisco, the rest of the United States, Canada, and Mexico whenever Chinese people were abused. For many years, it was the primary spokesman for the Chinese government in the United States. Its current headquarters was built with relief money from China after the earthquake in 1906.

Ironically, as a result of its political and legal victories, Six Companies has lost some power, since Chinese Americans now have access to the broader legal and political system. Most of Six Companies' energy is now devoted to charitable and educational activities in the community, though it is still capable of doing political battle.

Another function of associations was to provide cemeteries and burial expenses for the poor. The Chinese believed that the souls of the dead wandered endlessly if their bones were not returned to their ancestral burial grounds in China. For sanitary reasons, the bodies were buried for about six months, until decomposition was complete. The bones were then scraped clean and returned to China for permanent burial. Associations also provided medical services and free passage for the elderly and ill who wanted to return to China. Associations frequently accumulated large sums of money from their activities as labor brokers and from membership fees. For the most part, they operated on the honor system in terms of financial accountability.

CHAPTER 10
WAVERLY PLACE

Waverly Place is such an eclectic mix of niche businesses and unique retail outlets that many visitors do not even notice the presence of the family associations. You will see what I mean as we walk down the street.

To reach Waverly Place, walk down the hill on Sacramento from Stockton, or uphill from Grant. Pause at the corner of Sacramento and Waverly Place before walking down the east side of the street. Across the street, at 855 Sacramento, is the Chinatown YMCA.

Waverly Place is the most picturesque street in Chinatown. Often called the "street of painted balconies," it reminds many visitors of the French Quarter in New Orleans. Waverly was called "Fifteen Cent Street" because that was once the price of a haircut. Barbers, with their basins, set up on the sidewalks. There are still a few barber and beauty shops along this street. Before the Chinese Revolution in 1911, men had to wear queues, or braided hair. This practice was imposed by the horse-loving Manchu rulers. Queues were a sign of subjugation, and it was treasonous to not have one. Losing his queue meant that a man could not return to China. Each barbershop displayed a red and green stand holding a basin as a sign of its trade. The haircuts were more like shaves, as the hairlines were shaved back an inch or more. Most workingmen coiled their queues under their hats.

Across the street from the church, facing Waverly, but officially at 816 Sacramento, is **Clarion Music Center,** a unique music store. Clarion sells exotic instruments from China and many other countries. You can find simple folk instruments like tongue drums, ankle kettles, clay drums, *gogo* gourd thumb pianos, and *dizi* (purple bamboo flutes). You can also find more sophisticated instruments, like *kena* (Andean flutes that Anais Nin made famous), *ekwe* (Nigerian log drums), *taiko* (Japanese drums of the *Flower Drum Song* and the cherry blossom festival), and myriad stringed instruments like *liu ye quin* (Chinese mandolins) and *san xian* (Chinese banjos). Stop in and get a schedule of their public music performances.

The Clarion Music Center

Downstairs in the Clarion is where Chef Sammie Louie started his Chinese American Cooking School. He taught Chinese immigrants how to cook American style, which enabled them to find jobs in hotels and restaurants here and all over America. Louie remains a dedicated member of the community. This location is where my older brother, Barry, first served as executive director of the Chinatown Youth Center, from 1971 to 1972.

Points of Interest

Also on Waverly Place is the back entrance of the grand **Four Seas Restaurant**. Its main entrance is at 731 Grant Avenue, but if your tired legs do not want to go up over thirty steps, walk over to Clay and Waverly, and enter on the street level.

Waverly Place is home to numerous Chinese fellowship groups, printers, travel agencies, dentists, herbalists, beauty shops, electronic repair shops, and laundries. At 56 Waverly, an extension branch of **Armstrong University** offers courses in herb and physiotherapy.

The **Tien Hau Taoist Temple**, at 125 Waverly, honors the Goddess of the Heaven and the Sea. It is a celestial climb, up three flights of steep stairs.

Wonder Food, at 133 Waverly Place, has elaborate wedding cakes in its window display. The cakes are no different from American cakes. They also sell a variety of snacks such as pastries and cookies. Inside, older men study the *Daily Racing Form* while having tea, as younger men watch television.

The **Utopia Cafe**, at 139 Waverly, specializes in claypot dishes and a long line of trendy tapioca drinks, including watermelon, papaya, taro root, and red bean. Locals order from a wall menu written in Chinese. If you get friendly with the management, perhaps they will guide you away from the Americanized tourist dishes. You may wish to stop here for a quick lunch or for a refreshing beverage.

The **Pot Sticker**, at 150 Waverly Place, offers Hunan cuisine, assorted dumplings such as potstickers, and noodle dishes.

Waverly Place

First Chinese Baptist Church

The First Chinese Baptist Church at 15 Waverly Place provides a good example of the role of Christianity in the Chinese community. Founded in 1880 by Dr. John Hartwell, a former missionary to China, the church has been at this location since 1888. The congregation initially had nine members and met in rented quarters by Portsmouth Square. The church had programs for women and children, and taught many young men to speak English. The church currently has a membership of about 500, and carries out an extensive and comprehensive program for members in Chinese and English. They partner with the City College of San Francisco to teach English, and the church runs a six-week summer day camp for one hundred of Chinatown's community children.

Today, the First Chinese Baptist Church is easy to spot as its clinker bricks stick out from the façade. These are hallowed bricks, for they survived the 1906 earthquake. The recycled, burnt bricks from that great tragedy were laid into the new church building so that we might remember the earthquake. Before the church bought this property, the site had been home to a house of ill repute. Its flat roof was originally peaked, and the pitch line can still be seen on some interior walls.

The church has a beautiful sunken sanctuary, designed by Ed Sue, and marvelous stained glass windows. Many current Chinese American San Franciscans learned to speak English here. Many also learned to play American games like basketball on the playground directly behind the church. The mural on the outside wall of the church, by artist Jim Dong, depicts the old game of soapbox derby, but with a dragon boat soapbox.

The larger mural on the wall opposite the church, by John Kusakabe and Eliza Wee with help from seven other artists, depicts the traditional playground equipment of Chinatown, featuring high poles for the acrobatic game of leap tag. Completed in 1998, the mural commemorates the good fortune that no one was killed when a shooting took place at the adjoining Chinese playground that same year.

First Chinese Baptist Church

CHAPTER 11
SACRAMENTO STREET

As we reach Sacramento Street on our walk down Waverly Place, we will detour to visit some of the infrastructure that has propped up the community for over a century.

Sacramento Street is best known as *Tong Yun Guy*, which translates to "Chinese People Street." This was the first street where Chinese were allowed to rent rooms. My uncle, Henry Chew, and one of my former tour leaders, George Mew, were born and grew up in the same building at 725 Sacramento Street. George came from a large family, and, in the 1920s, living conditions were very cramped. When a family moved out of a unit, his moved in. Eventually, the Mew family took over the entire building. Back then, Chinese children were not permitted to attend public school with white children. Most of the Chinese youth went to St. Mary's Catholic school or to a public school established for Chinese—Commodore Stockton School, now named Gordon Lau School.

It was not uncommon for children to attend American school in the morning, followed by Chinese school in the evenings. George, for example, went to St. Mary's school on Clay and Stockton and then to a Chinese language school operated by a district association every night from 5:00 PM to 8:00 PM. George and his wife Martha have a daughter, Georgina, who was my classmate in college and is married to my high school friend, Arnold Chew.

Chinese School

As in San Francisco's Chinatown, children growing up in Oakland's Chinatown in the mid-1950s often went to American school in the morning as well as Chinese language school in the late afternoons and evenings. Chinese schools were developed to give the children a Chinese education so that they could return to China with knowledge of their language and culture. In fact, many children returned to China as bilingual business and professional people and contributed greatly to the country's development. My siblings and I attended Chinese language school a few blocks away from home at the Chinese Community Center. Today, we still speak Chinese with Mother, although it may sound fractured to her ears.

As discussed earlier in this book, we helped at our family restaurants as best as we could, from elementary school through our high school and college years. My mother didn't share my excitement at being accepted into the University of California at Berkeley, for it distanced me from working at our Bamboo Hut restaurant in Hayward, an hour's drive from Berkeley. I was expected to help out on weekends and holidays. My brothers and I worked at the restaurant in various shifts, and we were able to maintain good enough grades to graduate.

In San Francisco's Chinatown, the Nam Kue Chinese School, at 755-765 Sacramento, was established in 1925. It was created and operated by the Fook Yum Tong district association. After the 1906 earthquake, Chinatown had ceased to be a bachelor-type society and, for the first time, enjoyed a large number of children. Chinese Central High School at 827 Stockton Street, next to the Six Companies Benevolent Association, was the first community-operated Chinese school in San Francisco, opening in 1884.

The Nam Kue Chinese Language School

Asian Week Newspaper

Asian Week, 809 Sacramento Street, is the national English-language weekly newspaper for the Asian Pacific American community. It covers everything of importance and interest in the Asian American culture. During the Lunar New

Year period, *Asian Week* is the foremost newspaper for information regarding the new year traditions, foods, and, of course, the Lunar New Year parade.

Chinatown YMCA

The Chinatown YMCA, 855 Sacramento Street, was and still is a popular gathering place for young boys and men in the community. Today, the YMCA welcomes women to participate in their many programs. The YMCA offers a full range of activities for its members and visitors, including basketball, yoga, ballroom dancing, ballet, *tai chi*, cooking classes, swimming, and exercise programs. Additionally, the YMCA offers its annual Spring Break Day Camp and Summer Youth Program. The YMCA was organized in 1911 to provide recreational and educational programs for the young men of the community, and has been doing a great job ever since. One of my first Wok Wiz tour leaders, George Mew, recounts that he was once thrilled to win a swimming pool pass for correctly defining the word "initiative." Being able to use the pool meant that he could take a shower, an unaccustomed luxury, because there were no bathing facilities in his home down the street.

Chinese Chamber of Commerce

The Chinese Chamber of Commerce, 728-730 Sacramento Street, was established in 1908 as a compromise to settle a bitter economic feud between the Sam Yup and Say Yup district associations. The Sam Yups were merchants from the areas closest to Canton, while Say Yup people were laborers and restaurant employees from the southern area of the Pearl River delta. As a result of the feud, many Chinese businesses went bankrupt. Today, the Chamber is considered the most powerful political arm in the Chinese community, and it continues to be very active in the cultural and economic life here. Each year it co-sponsors the Miss Chinatown U.S.A. Pageant and the Lunar New Year parade. Wok Wiz supports the Chamber by buying at least one hundred parade tickets every year, and we offer Lunar New Year walking tours and dining programs throughout the glorious day.

The Donaldina Cameron House

The Donaldina Cameron House is located at 920 Sacramento Street. A unique woman, Donaldina Cameron was a missionary who helped young Chinese immigrant girls who were smuggled into the United States and bought and sold in the "yellow slave trade," as it became known in the 1870s. Originally called the Occidental Mission Home for Girls, this Presbyterian mission safe house opened its doors for Chinese women and girls in distress in 1897, when Ms. Cameron began working there as a sewing teacher. She stayed for over forty years, dedicating her life to missionary work, rescuing young women trapped in a life of slavery or prostitution. In 1947, Cameron House became a youth center for the Chinese community. Today it serves urban youth and families, offering leadership development, peer group counseling, crisis intervention, and much more.

Ms. Cameron's work will never be forgotten—and certainly not by my family. She and her staff helped my mother when she was detained on Angel Island in 1940, comforting her and other newcomers, while teaching them skills such as sewing and arts and crafts. When I took Mother back to Angel Island in 2001, she saw a picture in the museum of a woman she recognized as Katherine Maurer, an assistant to Ms. Cameron. Our father was once a cook for the Cameron House on special occasions, and as a favor to him, Donaldina Cameron personally escorted our mother off of Angel Island to meet him.

The Cameron House also greatly influenced the life of Wok Wiz tour leader Dorothy Quock. She explains, "I was born and grew up in San Francisco's Chinatown in a welfare family of eight children. By the time I was a fifth grader, my mother was a widow. So it was quite timely for me when the Presbyterian Church sponsored Donaldina Cameron House, which began its youth program in 1947. I was among the first young people participating. What a privilege when I met Miss Donaldina Cameron at an event there, honoring her before she died in 1968. I can still hear my mother in her frustrated times saying to me, 'Might as well move your bed there,' because Cameron House became my second home during my teens. I will be forever grateful for the Donaldina Cameron House and its staff, who gave me opportunities and experiences through the social services, leadership development, youth programs, and community advocacy. They not only laid out moral and ethical values, but they provided interpersonal skills and tools that helped me become a socially responsible, caring citizen, able share my enriched life to better the world." What a wonderful tribute from one great woman to another.

CHAPTER 12
CLAY STREET

Chinese Historical Society of America

The Chinese Historical Society of America's (CHSA) Chinese American National Museum and Learning Center is located at 965 Clay Street. Chinatown's most comprehensive museum is one block north and parallel to Sacramento Street. The CHSA is located in Chinatown's landmark YWCA building, designed by the famed Julia Morgan. For locals and visitors, young and old, this is an important stop in Chinatown, as history comes alive through lectures, art exhibitions, seminars, workshops, classes, and youth programs. There are internship and volunteer programs for students and community members, storytelling hour for kids, and a resource center for educators to develop curriculum related to Chinese America.

Incorporated in 1963, the CHSA was the first such Chinese American historical society in North America. Open to the public, the museum and learning center preserves cultural items and artworks that have direct reference to the history of the Chinese in the United States, and showcases a collection of over fifty thousand artifacts about Chinese America. For more information, visit their Web site: www.chsa.org or call 415-391-1188.

The Chinese Historical Society of America Museum

CHAPTER 13
THE FEAST WITHIN US

Dim Sum and Chinese Cuisine

Asians in general and Chinese in particular have always placed great importance on the dinner table. We spend a much higher percentage of our income on food than other people do, and we often judge hosts by the generosity of their tables.

Chinese cuisine is the oldest and among the healthiest. Because most Chinese are lactose intolerant, butter and cream are not involved in cooking. Our fats come mostly from what nutritionists now call "the good cholesterols." Take that for what it is worth. After all, medicine is the softest of the sciences, and nutrition is the melted ice cream of medical science. One decade's breakthrough discovery is usually taboo in the next decade, which explains why the Chinese do not get excited about food fads; most of our great dishes are hundreds of years old.

After conducting Chinatown tours for two decades, I have learned that most visitors come looking for a more authentic Chinese dining experience than they might find back home. To do this, they must overcome some bad myths about Chinese cuisine.

The first myth is that we eat "weird food." The Chinese do not eat snakes and civets any more than Americans eat alligators. At Wok Wiz, we have tried, sometimes in vain, to introduce certain new foods to guests on our tours. I always encourage a tasting, or at least a look at some dishes, without prejudice or disgust. A proud chef needs an open palate—a willingness to try anything. And in these times of ethnic, racial, and political polarization, new foods can open minds. Let us pray that the history of tolerance is moving in a positive direction. I promise though, no snakes and no civets.

The second myth about Chinese food is that the food in Chinese restaurants in Middle America is authentically Chinese. Untrue. Most people who come on our tour are happy to learn what authentic food is, while others may try what we offer, but still go home considering sweet and sour to be authentically Chinese. Sweet and sour, fortune cookies, and dozens of other familiar dishes were invented in America, mainly to please the sweet tooth of non-Asian customers. They have very little in common with classic Chinese cuisine.

Chinatown is divided into several different regional styles and into two basic café services—*dim sum* and dinner. Although Cantonese (southern) cuisine is predominant, Chinatown restaurants are as various as the regions of China. Though generalizations are dangerous, it is useful for visitors who do not like spicy foods to avoid Hunan and Szechuan restaurants, and for those looking for serious adventures to try places that do not have English-language menus.

Bernice Fong explains the ways of ordering Chinese food. See the menus written in Chinese at the New King Tin on Washington Street

The Art of Pointing

Dim sum is uniquely Chinese. The art form was introduced during the Sung Dynasty (AD 960—1279). The news quickly spread throughout China and eventually to the rest of the world. Once a brunch and lunch event, today *dim sum* is consumed around the clock, everywhere from five-star hotels to humble dives and home dinner parties. In most places, it is a veritable buffet on wheels, with restaurants offering as many as fifty different, small plates. *Dim sum* is most lavish on weekends, although business lunches make it popular all week. In some restaurants, carts wheel by tables and offer a choice of items. Other restaurants have you choose from a menu, and then cook to order.

Dim sum is served with tea in Chinese/Asian restaurants around the world. Literally, *dim* (pronounced "deem") translates to "point" and *sum* to "heart," so loosely it means "heart's delight" or "point to the heart." *Sum* may be more poetic, but *dim* is the word that gets the job done. I like to say that you "point to what you want, eat until your heart is happy and full." There are no menus in most *dim sum* restaurants, so you point to the dishes you want as carts are wheeled by your table piled high with small stainless steel, bamboo, or plastic steamers full of mouth-watering dumplings. This can frustrate first-time *dim sum* diners, especially if the containers are covered.

Even for newcomers who speak fluent Chinese, the art of *dim sum* may not come easily. Smile and look puzzled, and perhaps you will get help. If not, just start pointing and you will most likely be happy, or at least entertained. Be careful not to strain your neck struggling to keep pace with the carts, which seem to come from all directions. Surprisingly, in all my years of eating *dim sum*, I have yet to see a cart crash! This is really a mobile cafeteria where you sit still and the food comes to you.

Each steamer contains three or four dumplings made of tasty minced pork, shrimp, other seafood, chicken, or beef, steamed buns with chicken, or Chinese roast pork sausage. Another cart displays unique treats such as braised and stuffed bell pepper, braised duck and chicken feet, and lotus leaves stuffed with chicken and pork with sticky rice. Another cart shows off dessert treats, such as custard tarts, sesame balls, Chinese almond pudding, and sweet cakes. It is an incredible sight. Sharing *dim sum* with a group of relatives and friends is considered a social event. As the size of the group increases, order more food! For the total experience, add a couple of platters of stir-fried *chow mein* (pan-fried noodles) or *chow fun* (rice noodles), fresh steamed Chinese broccoli, and always end the *dim sum* luncheon with something sweet, like sesame balls or custard tarts. The waiter will mark your bill as you select dishes, and your final bill will include a set fee for tea.

A teahouse visit should be a relaxing time, so do not rush. If you are in one of the gigantic *dim sum* restaurants, the carts that seem to be whirling all around quickly circle the dining room, wheel into the kitchen for a refill, and return. Hint: sit by the kitchen and be the first to see what comes out!

In a Chinese Teahouse

As the noon hour approaches and our tour groups have spent over two hours learning about the history, culture, people, and food of Chinatown, we are usually ready for lunch. At the restaurant, we begin with a cup of tea. We usually share two types—an oolong or jasmine, and a stronger *pu-erh* with chrysan-themum flowers. The steamed dumplings come first—usually three or four varieties—followed by sticky rice stuffed in a lotus leaf package, and perhaps a personal favorite: young chives and shrimp potstickers. We then change plates to enjoy a savory beef *chow fun* (a platter of seasonal vegetables) and, last but not least, a traditional Chinese dessert.

Big sister Maggie Pavao shares Yank Sing's Mango Pudding with baby sister Stella, as Pau Pau Shirley watches.

Dim sum is still one of the best bargains in the world of dining out. However, *dim sum* has become more cosmopolitan. For a very upscale, unforgettable *dim sum* experience, I sneak out of Chinatown to the Yank Sing restaurant, located a block south of Market Street at 101 Spear Street, in the historic Rincon Annex. Yank Sing has over seventy-five types of *dim sum*, and is creative and play-ful, changing the menu with the times and trends. They were one of the first restaurants to make snow pea tendril dumplings—my personal favorite. Their prices are higher than most *dim sum* houses, but worth every bite.

Menus at world-class *dim sum* restaurants, like San Francisco's Yank Sing and Honolulu's Indigo, have added exciting and creative variations that expand *dim sum* into Pan Pacific fusion cuisine. In addition to its forty-item traditional menu, Yank Sing has a Creative Collection, which is revised monthly. Chicken and tarragon-stuffed mushrooms are an obvious example, since tarragon is not a Chinese herb. Yank Sing borrows soft shell crabs with chilies from Thailand and curried avocado from Japan and India. Chef Glenn Chu, owner of Indigo, offers a mouth-watering sesame ball filled with heavenly duck. Sesame balls are traditionally a *dim sum* dessert item, so Chef Glenn has taken it to another planet of delicious goodness. Shanghai 1930 takes me over the moon with their twist on two kinds of sesame balls—one filled with gooey, sumptuous chocolate, and another slathered with yummy, sticky peanut butter.

Yank Sing's famous and unique goldfish-shaped shrimp dumplings.

Now that the walking part of our virtual tour is complete, we will sit down for a virtual feast. You can find these dishes at many of the fine Chinese restaurants and teahouses we have visited on our journey.

Dim Sum Delights

With a minimum of twenty-five *dim sum* offerings at every teahouse, you can easily eat yourself silly. Here is a guide to some of the most popular *dim sum* items. *Dim sum* on!

Char Sil Bow: Steamed pork bun. One version is baked to a golden brown.

Char Sil* or *Ha Cheung Fun: Rice noodles with roast pork or shrimp steamed in a roll, served cold or fried.

Chern Goon: Spring Rolls (or Egg Rolls).

Don Todd: Custard egg tart.

Faw Op: Roast duck.

Fun Gor: Combination of pork, mushrooms, and bamboo shoots in wheat wrapper.

Gee Bow Gai: Paper or foil-wrapped chicken.

Ghow Nom: Beef tripe.

Gai Bow: Steamed chicken bun.

Gai Guerk: Braised chicken feet.

Chicken feet, anyone? Tour leader Alberta Chinn offers a foot to Shirley,
but the Wok Wiz has quite a few in her steamer basket.
Photo by Christina Koci Hernandez/San Francisco Chronicle

Ghow Yuk Sil Mi: Steamed beef dumpling.

Gwah Tip: Potstickers, a northern Chinese dumpling with a filling made of ground pork and cabbage, pan-fried on one side and steamed. Dip into a mixture of rice vinegar, chili, and sesame oil.

Har To See: Shrimp Toast. Minced shrimp and water chestnuts, spread on bread and deep-fried.

Har Gow: Steamed shrimp and bamboo shoot in a wrapper of wheat starch that is translucent when cooked.

Jin Dooey: Sesame seed ball filled with lotus or sweet bean paste.

Leen Yoong Bow: Sweet lotus seed steamed bun.

Lo Bok Go: Turnip cake.

Lot Jui Ha: Stuffed green bell peppers, filled with shrimp and topped with black bean sauce.

No Mi Gai: Lotus leaf stuffed with sticky rice, chicken, pork, and shrimp. The leaf imparts an interesting flavor to the ingredients in somewhat the same way a cornhusk flavors a *tamale.*

Op Guerk: Braised duck feet.

Seen Jook Guen: Bean curd skin rolls.

Seen Jook Guen: Fried, then steamed bean curd skin rolls.

See Jup Pai Gwut: Steamed black bean and garlic spareribs.

Sil Loong Bow: Succulent and delicate pork dumplings.

Sil Mi: Steamed pork or shrimp-and-pork dumpling with a wrapper made of thin wheat flour dough.

Stuffed Tofu: Triangles of fried tofu (bean curd) filled with minced pork.

Woo Tow Gaw: Deep-fried mashed taro root rice cakes with meat stuffing.

TV Chef Joey Altman and Shirley enjoyed lots of Yank Sing dim sum after a Bay Café taping.

In addition to *dim sum*, here are some recommendations for pleasing entrees.

Cheung Meng Mein: Long-life noodles, a "must" to celebrate birthdays.

Choy Sum Gai Kow Chow Fun: Chinese baby greens with chicken *chow fun*.

Dow Mil: Snow pea tendrils.

Gai Lon Ghow Yuk Chow Fun: Chinese broccoli with beef *chow fun* (rice noodles).

House Special *Chow Mein:* Most often, this *chow mein* is a platter of pan-fried noodles with a combination of shrimp, chicken, beef, and greens.

Ho Yow Gai Lon: Chinese broccoli with oyster sauce.

Jook: Rice congee, served plain or with different ingredients, such as thousand-year-old egg, lean strips of pork, topped with green onions and Chinese parsley (cilantro).

Peking (a.k.a. Beijing) Duck: Sometimes sliced tableside, served with steamed buns, hoisin sauce, slivers of green onion, and sprigs of fresh Chinese parsley (cilantro).

Sing Jow Chow Mi Fun: Singapore Noodles. Bean threads or stir-fried with shrimp, slivers of roast pork, green onions, with a curry seasoning.

At three years of age, Maggie Pavao is a regular at Yank Sing. She loves the Steamed Pork Buns and Sticky Rice in Lotus Leaf.

How to Order in a Chinese Restaurant

Important tips:

- Check out the clientele. If a restaurant is dominated by Asians who are dining happily, you're in the right place.
- If most of the menus are written in Chinese, that is a good sign.
- The food should not look too shiny or have a greasy appearance.
- The food should not contain MSG. Monosodium glutamate, long considered a food enhancer, is unhealthy. If you get headaches after eating Chinese food, you may be allergic to MSG.
- The food should look and be fresh.

Rice plates: A plate of steamed rice is served with your choice of toppings, such as broccoli beef, curried shrimp, barbequed pork, barbequed pork with scrambled egg, tiger prawns with scrambled egg, roast duck, black bean sauce spareribs, and, my favorite, braised beef stew Chinese-style.

Dinner for four: Take your time to plan your meal. Make it as balanced a menu as possible. Order at least four items to share by putting all the food in the center of the table on a "lazy Susan" as seen below. Consider ordering food that you are not familiar with. Start with a "soup of the day," which usually is not *won ton* soup. Order a steamed, rather than fried, fish; a claypot filled with vegetables and pork; a sizzling platter of beef in a spicy sauce; a tofu and greens special; and, of course, rice. When crab is in season, order a fresh Dungeness crab cooked with ginger and green onions, and ask for the Chinese vegetable of the day. Or, look around and see what other diners are enjoying, and point to it.

At Yee's Restaurant, a very happy Kevin Krull waits to dig into this mass of food on the "I Can't Believe I Ate My Way Through Chinatown!" tour. (Photo courtesy of Clifford Dunn.)

Specialty Chinese Foods

There are over one hundred restaurants in Chinatown. If travel is to be mind-expanding, you must open your mouth to new experiences. After all, the tongue bone is connected to the brain bone. Here are some key specialty food items used in our family dinners, celebratory meals, and multiple-course banquets:

Abalone Soup Ironically, abalone is the symbol of abundance. Because the California abalone is endangered, the traditional abalone soup almost always uses canned abalone. When the fresh kind is available, expect to pay up to a hundred dollars for a bowl. The soup is made with a rich chicken stock, thinly sliced abalone, Chinese black mushrooms, and napa cabbage. Some places add a raw egg to the soup pot right before serving it.

Bird's Nest Soup Alas, the swiftlet bird is also making its way to the endangered species list. This tiny bird is found in Thailand and other parts of Southeast Asia where it lives in dark caves and makes its nest out of its own gummy saliva. Nest harvesters go into the cave and pry the nests from the walls. I have seen gift-size boxes that cost five thousand dollars. As a kid, I did not like its flavor. As an adult, I know that little birds lose their homes, so I cannot bear to eat it.

Bitter Melon in Black Bean Sauce *Foo gwa* is an acquired taste. As a kid, I remember wrinkling up my nose whenever my parents placed a platter of this at the dinner table. Now I enjoy eating it because I know the bitter melon is good for me. Often touted for its health benefits, bitter melon helps regulate blood sugar levels. In the market, a bitter melon looks like a cucumber gone very wrong. It is usually about eight inches long, pale to dark green with what looks like pock marks. In cooking, it is cut in half length-wise and emptied of seeds. Then it is blanched for a few minutes and cooled to reduce the bitterness.

Durian Durian ranks with silky chicken for frequency of tourists wrinkling up their noses. This spiked fruit originated in Southeast Asia and looks like a ten-pound, wooden porcupine. Durians smell so foul that you are not allowed to keep them in hotel rooms, and most airlines forbid them passage. But once you get past all that, it is said to be a divine custard. I first tasted durian in juice form in Singapore, but still cannot get over the odor. However, judging from customers in Chinatown, durian is much loved. The thorny husk of the fruit ranges in color from green to brown, and when you get inside the fruit, it is soft as pudding.

Ginseng—for soup or cooking This very important root is considered a source of good energy and longevity, and millions believe in it. Ginseng is used to treat colds, high blood pressure, and headaches. I use it when I am fatigued, and before or after traveling to recompose my flow of energy. It is consumed as a tea and a raw root, but it is best with steamed chicken, mushrooms, and ginger in a soup bowl.

Hom Yee Jin Gee Yuk Steamed Salted Fish Pork Patty—I have been eating this dish since I was a little girl. It was often a part of our dinner menu, and I still like it. Some consider it "peasant food." Ground pork is topped with a small piece of salt fish, ginger, and green onions, and then steamed. I receive varying opinions from my Wok Wiz dining companions … very interesting.

Lo Han Jai. This is the traditional Buddhist stew for Lunar New Year, but this dish is also popular throughout the year. Symbolism plays a big role in this dish. Two ingredients, dried oysters and dried scallops, are often displayed in large, glass jars in herbal shops. The Chinese word for oyster is *ho see*, which sounds like "good news." The dried scallops are circular, representing the never-ending cycles of life. These are usually combined with rehydrated Chinese dried hair seaweed, *fot choy*. This dish is also a non-threatening way to consume black mushrooms and clouds ear fungus along with nearly a dozen fresh vegetables, bean curd sticks, tofu, and bean thread noodles (*sai fun*). The noodles are long, and thus represent a long life.

Lotus Roots The lotus is quite beloved, often a sign of purity. Images of Buddha rest atop a lotus flower. As children, my brothers and I used to play with our lotus root at the dining table, to the chagrin of our parents. It can be quite fibrous, so we liked taking bites and then forming "whiskers." In its natural form, the root resembles elongated potatoes that are connected together like beads. When cut into potato chip shapes, a pretty pattern of holes makes the slices resemble flowers, so chefs love them for presentations. The roots, crisp to the bite even when cooked, are used in soups, usually flavored with cuttlefish, chicken, or pork and dried tangerine peel, plus Chinese red dates. Sticky rice in a lotus leaf is a lovely presentation.

Lychee This delicious fruit is cute and fun to eat. It is about one and a half inches round, with a reddish, bumpy skin. Break off the top just enough for you to suck out the fruit and spit out the pit … sweet and juicy. Lychee is high in antioxidant Vitamin C and potassium.

Mooncakes Mooncakes are indeed shaped like the moon and are in wild abundance during the annual Chinese Moon (harvest) Festival. Cut a mooncake in half and the egg yolk in the center becomes two moons. Lotus root paste is often used in mooncakes to add enlightenment.

Peking Duck, also known as Beijing Duck. Remember when Caesar salad was made tableside with great fanfare? Well, Peking duck is still treated to such red carpet style in San Francisco. The duck comes to the table whole and it is carved and accessorized. The glazed skin is crisp and golden brown; the meat is tender. The duck is usually presented in bite-size pieces, but with its form preserved. Traditionally, the duck skin is served first, usually tucked into steamed buns, with a dollop of hoisin sauce and some julienned scallions. Next, the duck meat is served separately, sometimes stir-fried with fine vegetables, sometimes left alone. My favorite places in San Francisco for Peking duck are Shanghai 1930 and Yank Sing.

Preserved Duck Eggs My mother used to preserve duck eggs in an industrial-size mayonnaise jar. After placing the eggs carefully into the jar, she would add cold, salted water to cover the raw eggs. After a month or so, she would crack one open and mix it with slices of pork and then steam it. The cured egg white is water-like, and the yolk becomes bright orange, firm and whole.

Roast Pork (crispy skin) and Suckling Pig My sister Sarah and I both have cravings for *faw ghook* and once cooked it together—but apart. I prepared it in my home kitchen on the coast, while she was doing the same in her home across the Golden Gate Bridge. Pork bellies, with the skin on, are treated with salt, soybean condiment, dark soy sauce, sugar, garlic, and ginger before being cooked. The skin must be poked in the last fifteen minutes. Pig heaven.
There are always guests on our tour who gasp over the whole pigs that hang in King Tin, or Yee's Restaurant, and in many Chinese versions of a delicatessen. It is fun to watch a couple of cooks parade through the main dining area with a whole roasted pig hanging on a long, heavy stick between their shoulders. The pigs are slow-roasted over an open fire in a downstairs kitchen, leaving them with glistening, glowing skins and a red smoke ring inside the skin from the cooking process. The pig is then hung next to chopping boards, in full view of all. Before long, lines form with customers purchasing pig by the pound.

Shark's Fin Soup Once a staple at a Chinese banquet, certain types of shark are now on the endangered species list because of the popularity of the fins.

The fin on its own is rather tasteless, but it is miraculously absorbent. The dish depends on rich, double chicken stock and pieces of chicken. The fin is golden, translucent, and gelatinous, resembling noodles with spunk and also representing prosperity.

Silky Chicken Every time I walk by a Chinese fresh poultry market with my Wok Wiz tour groups, this question is posed: "Eeeek, what is *that*?!" The subject in query is "silky chicken," also known as "black-blue chicken." While many non-Asians are repulsed by blue food, this bird is revered in Chinese kitchens. This smallish bird has white feathers with dark eyes and beak. It has dark colored bones, meat, and skin. The chicken is usually used in shark's fin, abalone, and bird's nest soups, and it is good for blood circulation.

Squabs, deep-fried These little birds are deep-fried to a crisp. They are sometimes left whole, and sometimes cut into bite-size pieces, served with or without steamed buns. I have seen diners tear into the squabs, breaking them apart and dipping pieces into various sauces. You can also eat them without additional seasonings.

Whole Steamed Fish Whole steamed fish is almost always served at birthday dinners and other special celebrations, as it represents plenty of good luck. The fish head should face the guest of honor, who is always given the best part: the fish cheeks. The fish can be steamed simply with ginger and green onions, topped with a splash of hot oil and a flurry of Chinese cilantro, or steamed with fermented black beans, garlic, and ginger, and topped with Chinese cilantro. Some restaurants keep live seasonal fish in tanks for freshness. Black bass is a favorite, but preferences are regional and seasonal.

Whole Winter Melon Soup Most people remark that the winter melon resembles a watermelon. The large melon has a pale to dark green skin, usually with what appears to be a chalk covering. My father used to have several of these downstairs in our Bamboo Hut restaurant in Hayward. He saved them for banquets and special occasions. The top of the melon is cut off, and the seeds are removed. The cavity is filled with chicken broth, diced Chinese black mushrooms, dried scallops, bamboo shoots, fresh water chestnuts, ham, or chicken—all steamed to perfection. The melon is placed at the banquet tables and the melon becomes its own soup tureen.

At the Koi Palace in Daly City, the creative chefs prepare a marvelous version of Winter Melon Soup using spaghetti squash instead of the traditional winter melon.

CHAPTER 14
CELEBRATIONS AND TRADITIONS

When I was a child, I sensed a special day was around the corner whenever our mother busied herself at the sewing machine to make a new dress for me. Our kitchen would then be filled with sensational aromas of stir-fried dried shrimp; green onion; minced prawns; fresh water chestnuts; and earthy, Chinese black mushrooms—ingredients Mom used to make steamed or fried dumplings and pastries. She measured out wheat starch into our large, green mixing bowl and added boiling water, a little at a time. Then she would pound down on the flour and water with her hands to make dough. It amazed us that she never burned herself. Next, she would roll the dough into long, thin cylinders, cut them into even-sized pieces, and shaped them into little balls in the palms of her hands. Patiently, she'd scoop a tablespoon of filling into the center of each ball, and then deftly wrap them into even-sized little dumplings. Then she'd line the dumplings in rows on a flour-dusted cookie sheet. After they were cooked, we ate a few and she had some on hand for visitors or to take to our friends' homes.

Mom taught me how to make the dumplings. I think back to all the mothers and all the hours they must have spent making these wondrous little treats. It is no wonder that, to this day, I am most fond of making dumplings, especially Hand-hacked Seafood and Vegetable Potstickers. Whenever my daughter Tina comes over for dinner, we make the dumplings together, and now three-year-old Maggie helps and does a great job.

It seems as though we Chinese are always celebrating something. In between the American celebrations of birthdays, anniversaries, and national holidays, there is a stream of Chinese festivals with many customs and lots of word-play about tradition and food. Here are some of the most familiar Chinese celebrations.

LUNAR NEW YEAR

The Lunar New Year takes place between late January and early March, depend-ing on the lunar calendar, which is based on the phases of the moon. We celebrate for two full weeks. More food is consumed during the period of New Year festivities than at any other time. In addition to preparing vast amounts of traditional food for family and friends, food is also cooked for those close to us who have died. The foods that are set out for loved ones who have passed on are always their favorite dishes. Eventually, family members either eat the food or give it away. The house is cleaned thoroughly and bills are always paid up. On the day of New Year, we are not supposed to wash our hair lest we wash away good luck. Red clothing is conspicuous during this festive occasion because red is considered a bright, happy color, projecting a promise of a sunny and bright future. Children and unmarried friends, as well as close relatives, are given *lai see* (little, red envelopes with crisp dollar bills inserted, for good fortune).

Prior to the Lunar New Year's Day, we decorate our living rooms with vases of pretty blossoms, pots of blooming red azaleas, platters and bowls of oranges and tangerines, and a plate with eight varieties of dried sweet fruit. The number eight is considered the luckiest number of all, as the sound for eight is similar to the sound for prosperity. We Chinese are known for loving certain numbers, such as two, three, eight, and nine; we often request those for our telephone numbers and look for addresses containing those numbers when house-hunting. I take it further by making sure my airline flights and airplane seats contain suitable numbers. We place couplets—verses of happy wishes written on red paper—on walls and doors. These wishes sound better than the typical fortune cookie message. For instance, "May you enjoy continuous good health," and "May the Star of Happiness, the Star of Wealth, and the Star of Longevity shine on you," are especially positive couplets.

This holiday is shared by over a billion people in China and millions more in Chinatowns throughout the world. The atmosphere in our Chinatown is colorful and carnival-like. Street vendors set up tables on the sidewalks to sell products associated with the occasion: festive dried goods, fruits, plums, candy, fresh flowers, plants, and red envelopes in a range of sizes—always decorated with calligraphy or characters in gold. The already-crowded streets along Stockton and Grant and the side streets are jammed, as competing nursery trucks park and sell, on the spot, flowering plants and colorful blossoms of quince or peach that seem to reach to the heavens. I enjoy stepping back to soak in the energy of the day as Chinatown celebrates this magnificent time.

In the traditional family, there are many rituals. Although born in America, I know my roots and understand exactly how I am expected to behave. To visit my mother, I dress in an attractive, bright outfit and speak in an upbeat, positive manner. It is believed that appearance and attitude during New Year's set the tone for the year. I bring a bag of the brightest oranges and tangerines I can find, and the tangerines must have leaves intact. A red envelope with lucky money is placed in the bag. Our mother will give back half the fruits to me and tuck in lucky money envelopes. Etiquette dictates that you must bring this bag of fruit with *lai see* inserted whenever you visit family or friends during the two-week-long celebration. Tangerines with leaves intact assure that your relationship with others remains secure. For newlyweds, this also represents the branching out of the couple into a family with many children. You can choose the interpretation that best suits your hopes and dreams.

Special New Year Food

The two-week celebration of Lunar New Year is our number-one rationalization for overeating. Almost every dish has symbolic meaning—either long life, happiness, or good fortune. A vegetarian dish is traditional, as nothing should be killed on the first day of the year. Since the Cantonese word for oysters sounds like "good news," we eat oysters. Noodles represent longevity and are essential on New Year's Day and on birthdays. Seaweed hair, *fot choy*, means success and luck. Gingko nuts resemble little pieces of gold. Chicken is essential, as the Chinese word for chicken sounds like "goodness on earth." Fresh vegetables are popular as the color green represents growth, as do dollar bills! The Chinese word for a whole steamed fish sounds like "good luck." Served with head and tail on, it represents wholeness. Prawns are not only popular for their taste, but the word prawn in Chinese is *ha*. I made this up, but it sounds good: if you eat many prawns, you will laugh ("ha ha ha") and have wonderful joy, humor, and laughter in your life all year long. Okay, it may be lame, but it got me another dish at the table, right? The Lunar New Year two-week period is also the number one time of the year for non-Chinese tourists to visit Chinatown, so here are some information that will help you.

The New Year Parade

The culmination of the festivities is the spectacular New Year parade, presented annually by the San Francisco Chinese Chamber of Commerce and corporate sponsors. The Chinese New Year celebrations started in the 1860s as the early Chinese celebrated the start of a new year with great fanfare. Add that to the fever of the Gold Rush and you have a huge party. The parade is the largest Asian event in North America, and now there is even a greater draw: the weekend-long Flower Fair and Chinatown Community Street Fair attracts thousands of people into an already wildly busy Chinatown.

Over one hundred floats entertain more than five hundred thousand parade revelers who line the streets for hours in anticipation. It is worth staying for the entire parade, rain or shine. Marching bands come from near and far. School children dressed in traditional New Year clothing dance. Politicians and beauty queens wave to everyone. Dozens of lion-dance groups, stilt walkers, Chinese acrobats, and martial arts students perform. Corporate sponsors and groups vying for "best float" prizes are out to dazzle. Of course, special floats will feature the theme of the year's Chinese zodiac sign. It is indeed a spectacle to behold. Finally, a colorful, eighty-foot Golden Dragon designed in China and operated by fifty people weaves its way from the start of the parade at Market and Second to the reviewing stand area at Kearny and Clay Streets to an ear-popping, firecracker climax. It would not be a proper parade without the drums and firecrackers, since they combine to add to the revelry, and their loud sounds scare away the evil spirits. For more information, contact www. chineseparade.com. Best of all, my brother, Ben Fong-Torres, is a co-host for the KTVU-Fox Channel 2 broadcast of the parade. He has been co-host for over ten years and is at the start of the parade while I am busy with the Wok Wiz annual Lunar New Year Gala in the heart of Chinatown.

What's Your Sign?

Before the actual Lunar New Year's day, one of the questions I get the most is: "What's my animal year? How do I find out?" Just as people ask, "What's your sign?" when referring to the Western zodiac, many Chinese ask, "What is your animal year?" On our Wok Wiz tours, as an icebreaker, we ask people the month and year of their birth so we can identify the animal under which they were born on the Chinese calendar. Whether or not one believes in astrology, it is fun to learn what animal your birth date represents.

According to Asian legend, almost five thousand years ago, Buddha called together all the animals of creation for a meeting. Only twelve creatures showed up. The first to arrive was the rat, followed by the ox, tiger, rabbit, dragon, snake, horse, sheep, monkey, rooster, dog, and finally, slowly but surely, the pig. For their loyalty, Buddha named a year after each one of these animals, in the order that they arrived.

Today, believers claim that one's personality and destiny are shaped according to which animal sign one is born under. A person born in the year of the Snake, for example, supposedly possesses great wisdom and beauty and is reflective, organized, and alert.

Whereas the cycle for the Western zodiac takes twelve months, the Chinese astrological cycle takes twelve years. For instance, Snake people were born in 1929, 1941, 1953, 1965, 1977, 1989, and 2001.

Of course, this is only an introduction to the field. Serious students of Chinese astrology, like their Western counterparts, devote a great deal of time and effort to the subject.

The Wok Wiz Family of Lunar New Year Animals

The Year of the Rat: My daughter, Tina, and her husband, Matt, were both born in 1972, the year of the Rat, but I prefer to say that Tina was born in the year of the cute Mouse. This is the first year in the cycle, a time for fresh beginnings and renewals. A Rat year is a good time to make new plans, launch businesses, get married, and begin a family. People born in the Rat year can be impatient, move around fast, and are quick to adapt to situations and new environments. Although Rats are thrifty, they are symbols of wealth because they always manage to find food, which is basic to survival, and if you have food, you are considered wealthy. 1924, 1936, 1948, 1960, 1972, 1984, 1996, 2008

The Year of the Ox: Those born in this year are often described as powerful and stubborn, not willing to make many changes or sacrifices once a decision is made. This year tends to be more traditional and conservative, and if agreements or contracts are being considered, have them signed in ink before the end of the Ox year. Following through and meeting deadlines are important to an Ox person. 1925, 1937, 1949, 1961, 1973, 1985, 1997, 2009

The Year of the Tiger: Tigers are fighters, powerful, aggressive, and rebellious. Artist-poet William Blake admired their awe-inspiring "fearful symmetry." Ancient Greeks called it charisma. Tigers are impulsive, which can be positive or negative depending on the situation. These beautiful animals can become hot-headed and will attack when their territory is invaded. 1926, 1938, 1950, 1962, 1074, 1986, 1998, 2010

The Year of the Hare: The rabbit is a soothing animal who arrived at Buddha's gathering after the tiger and before the magical dragon. Rabbits are reserved and shy, but when necessary are quick on the draw. They are persistent and keep going and going. Rabbits use diplomacy to get their point across and usually are kind-hearted and lovable. In Vietnam, where rabbits are rare, Rabbit's year becomes the year of the Cat. 1927, 1939, 1951, 1963, 1975, 1987, 1999, 2011

The Year of the Dragon: The Dragon is the flashiest and boldest member of the Chinese astrological family. During Lunar New Year parades, much ado is made about the arrival of the Dragon, which usually makes its entrance accompanied by extra loud drums and an overkill of firecrackers. The Dragon is very dramatic and exciting, so many Dragon people become actors and fashion designers. Dragons are the luckiest animals, and many people wait for a dragon year before beginning grand endeavors. 1928, 1940, 1952, 1964, 1976, 1988, 2000, 2012

The Year of the Snake: The Snake is a symbol of medicine. People born into a Snake year are thoughtful and contemplative and remain calm in troubled times. They tend to be on the quiet side and nurture long-term friendships through their patience and ability to communicate with little confrontation. Snakes are not considered lucky, and snakes are rarely depicted during their reign. 1929, 1941, 1953, 1965, 1977, 1989, 2001, 2013

The Year of the Horse: As the saying goes, "Healthy as a horse!" People born in the Horse year are tough, hardworking, well spoken, and competitive. Both graceful and swift, they can also be very emotional and impulsive, and are gamblers (at the horse races, perhaps?) This is a good year to keep a watchful eye on finances. 1930, 1942, 1954, 1966, 1978, 1990, 2002, 2014

The Year of the Sheep: Also called the year of the Goat, Lamb, or Ram. Sheep people are usually considerate, gentle, and wise. They do not rush and take their time to do things right. When things are not right, however, they will make a sudden change with little or no notice. Sheep people are quite content to be a part of the herd; they listen to others and observe, rather than being the life of a party. My first granddaughter, Maggie Sophia Pavao, born on October 16, 2003, is an adorable little lamb. 1931, 1943, 1955, 1967, 1979, 1991, 2003, 2015

The Year of the Monkey: Monkeys are intelligent, quick-witted, and playful. They possess great energy, are fast learners, and are prone to be successful in their endeavors. My brother Ben, a very successful writer, was born in the year of the Monkey. Further, a Monkey person is the center of attention at parties, ready to tell funny stories and amuse friends with jokes and tricks. Monkey people generally prefer the big city to rural areas. 1932, 1944, 1956, 1968, 1980, 1992, 2004, 2016

The Year of the Rooster: Proud and domineering, Roosters are great managers and leaders. They move fast and speak their mind to the point of being abrasive. They are ambitious, independent, and assertive. As bosses, they may be difficult to work with or satisfy, as they are particular and demand perfection. My mother was born in the year of the Rooster. 1933, 1945, 1957, 1969, 1981, 1993, 2005, 2017

The Year of the Dog: People born under the year of the Dog sign are generally friendly and sociable. They are loyal, faithful, and brave. They have ready smiles and are easy to get along with. They are faithful companions and devoted partners. On the other hand, Dog people can be suspicious and overly curious. Like dogs, they may enjoy hiding treasures. I am born in the year of the Dog and am known to be a rather friendly woman. We were blessed with two additions to our family in 2006: Stella Olina Pavao, Maggie's sweet little sister, born on April 26. Cousin Haden Berlinsky was born on October 13, into the year of the Dog. 1934, 1946, 1958, 1970, 1982, 1994, 2006, 2018

The Year of the Pig: The pig was the last animal to attend the meeting with Buddha because the pig had a hard time getting out of bed. Pig people tend to be on the quiet side and are easy to get along with at home and at work. They are generous with their time and friendship, and are good mediators. They may be easy-going to a fault, allowing people to take advantage of them. They can be homebodies and anchor themselves to a favorite spot. On the whole, it is an advantage to have Pig people on your side, as they believe in the good of others and are happy to give without expecting anything in return—except abstinence from eating pork, of course. We can all learn from Pigs. 1935, 1947, 1959, 1971, 1983, 1995, 2007, 2019

Shirley with Gene Burns and Pink Floyd guest on Dining Around with Gene Burns, *KGO-Radio, before being interviewed on Gene's show on the occasion of the year of the Pig celebration, 2005.*

TEA FOR YOU AND TEA FOR ME

"People drink tea for different reasons," says San Francisco's tea guru Roy Fong, who happens to be my cousin. We are drinking tea at his Imperial Tea Court, on the edge of Chinatown/North Beach. Roy continues, "People drink tea as a beverage to quench thirst, or for health purposes. Others drink tea as a form of meditation; the act of brewing tea in a ceremony or as a part of a tea service can be viewed as soothing and calming. Still others look at tea brewing and drinking as an art—the collection of tea wares and the search for the best tea at its earliest available time, become a lifetime quest."

In many ways, the Chinese appreciation of tea is similar to the love of fine wine in the West, both in its production and appreciation. In each case, the finished product is an expression of the soil and climate where it is grown, the time of year it is harvested, the plant variety, and the different processing techniques used. Similar to wine, the plants that produce tea come from years of careful cultivation. And the skill used to create the wide variety of taste sensations comes from years of tea crafting knowledge passed down from one generation to the next.

The same attention to detail in producing the tea can be applied to its appreciation. People in different regions have varying tastes for the product, some preferring black teas, others green or jasmine teas. And like wine, tea must be handled carefully to preserve its integrity. The color and particularly the aroma of each should be savored before drinking.

Tea Time

Chinese workers drink tea throughout the workday. Sharing social tea with friends and family at *dim sum* is very popular in southern China. We have no particular time of the day to drink tea. Sharing a cup of tea is an essential step in showing respect for a companion. A host brings tea to the table before food is served, and the guests may relax, knowing the tea will aid in their digestion. Most Chinese do not drink tea during the course of the meal. Green or oolong tea without milk or sugar is served at the beginning of the meal. After a meal, a stronger-flavored tea may be served to cleanse the palate.

Newcomers to Chinatown may experience a few teahouse rituals that require explanation. The tapping of fingers or knuckles on the table after tea is poured is an expression of thanks. This practice springs from the legend that Emperor Qian Long made an incognito visit to southern China during the eighteenth century. To preserve his anonymity, the emperor would occasionally pour tea for his manservant and other guests. Since the servant could not kowtow (bow) to the emperor, the servant invented the practice of tapping on the table with his knuckles to represent a kowtow.

Teapot lids are often tipped and left ajar at the teahouses as a signal to waiters to refill the teapots. Waiters also leave the lids ajar to signify that a table is ready to be cleared. Sometimes they use leftover tea and pour it on the table before wiping it clean, tea-clean.

Although there are countless varieties of tea, there are only three basic ways of processing the leaves after harvesting. The degree to which the leaves are fermented, or oxidized, determines if it will be a black tea, an oolong, or a green tea. Black tea involves the most complex process: fresh tea leaves are allowed to completely brown before they are fired, a process that creates its color and richer flavor. One pound of finished black tea takes four pounds of tea leaves. Green tea is the simplest process, involving no fermentation. Semi-fermented teas, like oolong, are full bodied and the most popular in Chinese restaurants. Most Chinese tea drinkers prefer green or oolong teas.

Chinatown offers a great opportunity to acquaint yourself with the pleasures of tea. If you have only tried the teas available at the supermarket, you are missing a lot. Some rules of thumb in choosing tea are to consider appearance, flavor, color, and aromatics.

Tea Distinctions

My good friend, Peter Luong, assisted with the information below. This will certainly be of value to our many Wok Wiz guests who consider a stop at the Red Blossom Tea Shop (www.redblossomtea.com) a highlight of our walk. Peter and his sister Alice welcome guests to return to their shop after our tour for further discussions and tastings.

True tea comes from the leaves of the camellia sinensis plant. Once picked, enzymes in the leaf will begin to turn it brown. This reaction is natural and will alter the color and flavor of the tea that is made from that leaf. Very simply:

Green Teas

- Tea leaves that are steamed or roasted to prevent any browning from occurring.
- Locks in the freshness of the tea leaf.
- Examples include Dragonwell, *Huang Shan Mao Feng*, and *Pi Lo Chun*.

Oolong Teas

- Tea leaves that are allowed to partially brown before roasting.
- Somewhere between a black and a green tea.
- Comes from four major areas: Taiwan, two areas in Fujian (Anxi and Wuyi), and Guangdong.
- Examples include *Tung Ting* and *Tie Kuan Yin*.
- *Pouchong* or *Baozhong* are very lightly oxidized oolongs, closest to green teas.

Black Teas

- Tea leaves are fully browned before roasting.
- Darker infusions.
- Examples include Keemun.

Pu-erh Tea
- Can be either "raw" or "finished."
- Raw = leaves are made into green tea and left to age.
- Finished = leaves are steamed and fermented.
- Comes from the southwestern Chinese province of Yunnan.
- When fresh, they are green teas; when fermented, they are made into a black tea, or if aged, the tea is green, oolong, or black.
- Pu-erhs are sold as loose leaves, in tea bricks, or teacakes.
- Add chrysanthemum blossoms to offset its very strong flavors.

White Tea
- Distinct varieties of camellia sinensis.
- Minimally or not at all browned.
- Steamed.
- Usually picked as young leaf buds.
- Examples include Silver Needle and White Peony.

Jasmine Tea
- Any tea that is scented with Jasmine flowers.

Tea Tips

Tea should be stored in a cool, dark area in tight containers to prevent loss of flavor and absorption of unpleasant flavors. Black teas retain their freshness the longest, and green teas are the most perishable. The beautiful, airtight tea containers sold throughout Chinatown are a decorative and functional way to preserve your tea. Stored in one of these containers, tea will keep its flavor up to two years.

There are nearly as many theories about how to make a good cup of tea as there are tea drinkers. The following works for me:

1. Unless you have large parties, stick to a small pot. Too much volume will often cause the leaves to stew and diminish the flavor. Large pots also slow

down the brewing process. Choose a pot that is comfortable to your hand and one that has a lid that will not fall off when you pour the tea. I am speaking from experience.

2. Choose a good quality tea. Quality tea tastes better and lasts longer. A pound of good tea will yield about a hundred cups, so tea is an inexpensive beverage even if you use the very best. Plus, you and your loved ones deserve to drink the best tea.

3. Never use hot water from the tap or water that has been standing in the pipes for long. It will taste flat and may contain chemicals or metallic flavors from the plumbing. Some purists will only use mineral water, although that may be going a bit too far.

4. Heat the pot with hot water before brewing the tea. This rinses the pot and will keep the tea hot longer when it is brewed.

5. Use one teaspoon of loose tea for each cup. If you are dealing with large volumes or prefer strong tea, add an extra teaspoon to the teapot.

6. Bring the water to a boil, but remove from heat the moment it begins to boil. If the water boils too long, it loses oxygen and tastes flat. Then let the water cool a bit before pouring over the tea. For those who want to experiment more precisely with temperatures, the Imperial Tea Court recommends the following temperatures: for green tea, 158°F or 70°C; for jasmine or light green oolongs, 176°F or 80°C; for black tea and *pu-erh* tea, 194°F or 90°C.

7. Brewing time varies with the type of tea, individual tastes, and the size of the teapot. Thirty seconds to one minute should be sufficient for green teas, while black teas may take longer.

8. Enjoy the color and aroma of your tea before drinking it. And, offer a toast. Here's to your health!

Lovely tea cups and tea sets on display at the Red Blossom Tea Shop.

CHINATOWN'S ALTARS, SIGNIFICANT CELEBRATIONS, AND FESTIVALS

In the home and business, altars are set up for people to pray for the deceased. Food is often placed there, alongside flowers and plates of oranges and other fruits. Incense burns as a form of sending messages to the heavens. In 2001, as I was doing some writing in my old office, a couple showed up at my door. Mr. and Mrs. Jeung walked in, and Mr. Jeung told me that when he was a child, which was more than sixty years ago, he and his family lived in what is now my office. He and his wife went on to tell me that 654 Commercial Street has had many lives. Indeed—it has been a sewing factory, a store, a flower shop, and a residence. For this reason, it is important to place a small altar on the ground level of my office for all the spirits who have resided or have somehow occupied my Commercial Street space in the past. It is a matter of respect. For the same reason, all Chinese temples (places of worship) have small altars placed on the ground level or on the street level right outside the main door.

The Kitchen God

Before the actual New Year, the Kitchen God returns to the heavens to give a report of the family's activities to the Jade Emperor. Many believers place a dab or two of honey on a picture image of the Kitchen God and burn it so that the smoke and incense transport his spirit to the heavens. The honey ensures he will only have good things to say. The family gathers for the opening of the New Year to share a dinner with the traditional foods, especially *lo han jai*, a vegetarian stew, and a whole fish to represent togetherness and abundance. The abundance of food means that our rice bowls will remain full throughout the year. Most of the food is prepared the day before so that no cutting is done on New Year's Day, for fear that one might "cut the luck of the New Year."

Birthdays

Significant birthdays, such as the sixtieth, seventieth, eightieth, ninetieth, and especially the hundredth are grand celebrations. The honored person may wish to have a big banquet or a simple one surrounded by close family members. The menu is often designed with entrees that symbolize long life and happiness. When our mother had her eightieth birthday dinner party, we made sure that we ordered "long life noodles" as the last course. Eating long noodles on your birthday means you will have a long and happy life. Whole chicken, *gai*, sounds like "good world" in Chinese, so it is lucky to eat chicken. Dried seaweed, *fot choy*, sounds like "prosperity."

Weddings

A traditional Chinese tea ceremony may take place after a wedding ceremony, at which time the bride is received into the family and showered with gifts of jade, pearls, and gold. She may then change into a traditional Chinese dress of embroidered silk, usually a brilliant red or yellow, sleeveless with a side slit and a mandarin collar. She also wears all the pieces of jewelry received at the tea ceremony. Nowadays, some brides hire bodyguards to accompany them to the formal banquet. According to banquet tradition, the bride, groom, and respective families sit at tables on a raised platform. On the wall, the character for double happiness is emblazoned in gold. The sumptuous banquet may include shark's fin soup, an expensive delicacy that represents prosperity—the golden color of the soup represents gold, long life, and the power and speed of a shark. Chinese banquets are often long and drawn out by speeches in both Chinese and English. Be prepared to make a whole evening or afternoon out of a wedding banquet experience.

Red Egg and Ginger Party

A Chinese baby's one-month birthday is usually celebrated with an afternoon luncheon at a teahouse. Today, however, the party often takes place after the baby is several months old, as there is no hard-and-fast rule. The baby is dressed up, and often wears gifts of jade, gold bracelets, and necklaces. Since the baby usually sleeps through this party, it is really a celebration for family and friends. In addition to the good food, it gives everyone a chance to meet the newborn child. Hard-boiled eggs (tinted in the lucky color red) and golden-colored, sliced, pickled ginger are always served to guests toward the end of the meal. The red eggs symbolize happiness and fertility, a renewal of life. The ginger adds an element of *yang* (warmth) to balance the *yin* (coolness).

We gave our daughter Tina such a party, and yes, she slept through most of it. Tina married Matt Pavao in 2001, and they blessed us with Maggie and Stella. In 2004, along with Tina's father, Richard Dong, and his wife, Marie Tso, we hosted a Red Egg and Ginger Party for our first granddaughter, Maggie Sophia Pavao. Sweet Maggie wore a pretty outfit and was a charming guest-of-honor, meeting over 250 guests. The party was held in my hometown, Oakland, at the Silver Dragon Restaurant, so the spirit of our father was surely with us. In 2007, we gave a similar party for baby Stella Olina at Yank Sing restaurant in San Francisco. The Red Egg and Ginger Party is always a happy and joyful occasion.

Four generations at Maggie Pavao's Red Egg and Ginger Party at the Silver Dragon Restaurant, Oakland. From left: Maggie's mother (Tina), baby Maggie, Shirley, and Shirley's Mother (Connie Fong-Torres).

Mid-Autumn Festival

The Mid-Autumn Festival is also known as the Moon Festival. Boxes of moon-cakes seem to fly out of Chinatown's stores in August or September each year. With great fanfare, the Chinese community celebrates the moon festival on the fifteenth day of the eighth month of the lunar calendar. The annual festival, second only in importance to New Year, is a time to give thanks for the bounty of the summer harvest.

Legend has it that when you look at the moon closely on this night, you may see a three-legged toad that was formerly a beautiful woman, or you may see a rabbit sitting under a tree.

Treat yourself to a slice of mooncake. Mooncakes are traditionally round and about three inches in diameter. They are filled with rich, usually thick and sweet lotus paste, red bean paste, or black bean paste. Most of the mooncakes contain a cooked, salted duck egg yolk in the center, so when you cut the cake in the middle, you see the moon. Caution: the egg yolk is often salty, and enjoying it may be an acquired taste. To impress those "in the know," present them a box of double-yolk mooncakes for double happiness.

During the Moon Festival Weekend, San Francisco's Chinatown is transformed into an extensive street festival. It begins with a grand parade, led by city dignitaries, school and community bands, and lion dancers. Hundreds of booths line Grant Avenue and side streets. You can find "Got Dim Sum?" T-shirts, contests for free gifts, and bargain prices on souvenirs and "must-haves." There are scheduled live performances throughout the day. Singers, martial art performers, and dancers add to the revelry of the Moon Festival celebration.

Chinese Funerals in Chinatown

Occasionally in Chinatown, you will hear a street band blaring or see police officers stop traffic to signify that a funeral procession is coming through. It begins with a white convertible carrying a portrait of the deceased, followed by the marching band. Sometimes the family members and close friends walk alongside the slow-moving hearse. If the deceased was a well-known member of the Chinese community, the hearse drives by his or her favorite places for a last visit to Chinatown. Play money is thrown on the street by the mourners to placate evil spirits that might bother the deceased in the afterlife. The surviving family members host a luncheon or dinner. Today, Chinese restaurants offer specific dishes for the occasion. After the funeral, you receive money, usually a dollar or less, in little red envelopes, to buy something sweet to eat to get rid of sad feelings.

Ching Ming Day

This is also known as Ancestors Festival or Grave-Sweeping Day. *Ching* translates to "pure" or "clean," and *ming* translates to "clear" or "bright." The *Ching Ming* Festival starts two weeks after the vernal equinox, which is around April fourth or fifth. It is similar to a rite of spring, when people begin to do more outdoor activities in the fresh, bright days of the new season. Families gather for *Ching Ming* rituals at the cemetery. They clean the headstone, weed the nearby area, and put out fresh flowers. Incense burning, followed by burning paper money is common, for some believe that money is necessary in the afterlife. Food is laid out at the grave, somewhat like a *dim sum* picnic. Out of respect to the deceased, members of the family take turns standing in front of the headstone to bow three times—once for the past, once for the present, and once for the future. Incense is always burning during these rituals because incense helps deliver offerings to the spirits, such as paper cars, paper eyeglasses, or other things they might need in the spirit world.

Festival of the Dead

Called *Yu Lan* in Chinese, this festival is celebrated on the fifteenth day of the seventh month. It is also known as the Feast of the Hungry Ghosts. Many Chinese believe in ghosts and spirits, and this festival resembles Halloween and the Day of the Dead (*Dia de los Muertos* in the Mexican culture). On this day, believers say the ghosts and spirits arise to return to earth, and the festival is devoted to the dead who are *not* one's ancestors. It is mainly to pacify the ghosts of the uncared-for dead and strangers—the forgotten. The ghosts are free to "let loose" and have a month of wandering around. It is similar to the *Ching Ming* day in some ways, as paper money, paper gifts of clothing, jewelry, cars, and fresh fruit and food offerings are left at the graves and altars for the dead.

Dragon Boat Festival

This festival is celebrated on the fifth day of the fifth moon of the lunar calendar, usually in late May or early June. Many consider it the third most important festival, after Lunar New Year and Autumn Moon Festival. It honors Chu Yuen, a prime minister of the Celestial Empire, who committed suicide by drowning in 288 BC. Though highly respected, he lost favor and became discouraged. A great reward was offered for the recovery of his body. Today's boat races use long and narrow dragon boats to represent the same boats used to search for Chu Yuen.

PHILOSOPHY, RELIGION, AND *FENG SHUI*

The Chinese revere their philosophers. Chinese art, architecture, food, medicine, and religion all have philosophical foundations. Most can be traced to Lao Tze, who was perhaps more legendary than historic. Some scholars believe that rather than being a real person, he represents a composite of several sages. His name means "old master."

Still, consensus legend holds that he was born in Hunan in 604 BC, making him an older contemporary of Confucius, living in wild days of violence and corruption. Fed up with complexities of urban life, he retired to the western frontier of China to write *The Book of the Way and of Virtue*, one of the world's great spiritual classics.

Taoism

Taoism teaches that a cosmic law governs the operation of the universe. By living in harmony with the laws of the universe, man is able to achieve true wisdom and enlightenment. The principle means of following Tao, "the way," is to not force things to meet your desires or expectations. The wise man learns from the example of water flowing around obstacles. Tao teaches that everything is in a constant state of change. Rigid attachment to anything, especially ideas, is fatal; flexibility results in renewal. "To bend is to maintain integrity."

Taoist thought holds that all changes occur in cycles. The classic Chinese text, the *I Ching*, is an analysis of the cyclic nature of change. Legend holds that it was written in prison by one of the founders of the Chou dynasty, Wen Wang, in 1133 BC, as a manual for divination. Confucius, who edited the book, described it as the greatest of all writing.

The concept of *yin* and *yang* is fundamental to Taoist thought. Essentially, *yin* represents the forces of nature that accumulate and conserve, while *yang* represents the forces of nature that expand or radiate. *Yin* is feminine, gentle, passive, and associated with calming water, the serene night, and the moon. *Yang* is masculine, bold, active, and associated with fire, daylight, and the sun. The concept originated with eight trigrams introduced by Emperor Fu Hsi. Trigrams consist of three lines, some of them broken (*yin*) and some continuous (*yang*). In the *I Ching*, Wen Wang doubled the number of strokes, creating sixty-four possible combinations of continuous and broken lines. Each combination represents some law of nature.

Taoists believe there are five elemental energies: water, wood, fire, metal, and earth. These energies roughly correspond to the seasons—with the exception of earth, which represents stability. Water, like winter, represents the extreme *yin* in which energy is stored and accumulated. Wood, like spring, represents the ultimate *yang* of expansive growth and renewal. Fire, like summer, represents a period of less expansive, but more sustained growth. Metal, like autumn, represents a period in which energy is drawn inward and conserved.

Physics verifies what Chinese mystics have taught for centuries: our world is made of countervailing energy, with pulses and rhythms. This applies not only to our biological makeup, but also to our behavior. Taoists believe that failure is as important as success, and that we should look on our setbacks as opportunities to learn and grow. Rather than following the rigid rules of society and religion, Taoists believe that enlightenment comes from an awareness of the cycles of the universe.

Confucius

The second foundation of Chinese philosophy is the writings of Confucius. Born in the state of Lu, now the province of Shantung (Shandong) in 555 BC, he was brought up in an impoverished environment by his young, widowed mother. He was self-taught and became a teacher himself at age twenty-three.

Confucius expounded an idealistic plan of five relationships to ensure unity in the family, as well as in the nation: ruler to subject; husband to wife; father to son; elder brother to younger brother; friend to friend. On a larger scale, Confucius believed that relationships between the emperor and his subjects were similar to those in the home, with the emperor ruling as a father of a large family. An ethical government where the leader sets good examples and where his subjects understand their roles results in a world of peace and tranquility.

Over almost fifty years, Confucius taught more than three thousand students. Confucius taught his students to revere learning, sincerity, and order. After his death, his influence spread to Japan and Southeast Asia through his followers. His philosophy served as an integral part of Chinese thought and morality for over two thousand years. Many Chinese have strongly challenged and rejected aspects of Confucianism that seem outmoded, such as its patriarchal treatment of women as subservient. Confucius died a frustrated and unhappy man, not realizing his dream to persuade the rulers of China to eliminate abuses of power and corruption.

It is important to distinguish Taoism the philosophy from Taoism the religion. The religious practices of Taoism evolved from the search for magic potions and immortality. This laid the foundation for Chinese medicine. Taoists also developed systems of meditation and physical exercise. The religion's founder was Chang Tao-Ling, who was born in AD 35. He claimed that Lao Tze descended from heaven. Chang concocted a potion that he claimed would cure many ills, and thousands flocked to him for treatment. His fee was five bushels of rice, which led to his being dubbed "the rice thief." Those not cured by him were told that their faith was insufficient. Somehow, Chang lived to age 122. He is usually depicted as an old man riding a tiger.

Taoism incorporated many beliefs from Chinese folk religion, such as animism—the belief that everything, animate or inanimate, has a spirit. The Taoists worship many gods. The religion includes a concept of hell, although it is a temporary one, more like Christian purgatory. Taoists are still led by descendants of Chang Tao-Ling. Taoist priests do not proselytize, but they are happy to explain their religion.

Buddhism

Buddhism is a major religion based on the teachings of Siddhartha Gautama, the "enlightened one" who lived more than 2500 years ago in northern India. Of the various stories about Buddha's youth, I prefer this one:

Prince Siddhartha was born son of King Shuddhodana and Queen Mahamaya. As a young man, he rejected the luxurious lifestyle of his family and became an ascetic—on his own journey to find truth. After years of wandering and meditation, he reached enlightenment and became a Buddha and started to teach. Buddha died at age eighty after spreading his word for more than half of his life.

Buddhism is often considered a practice rather than a religion, sharing the Golden Rule of "Do to others as you would have others do to you," with many religions. It preaches nonviolence, peace, and serenity. Buddha means to "show the way" so that followers learn to find their own truth.

Temples in Chinatown

Visitors are welcome in the Chinatown temples as long as they are respectful. Inside a temple, statues represent various gods and goddesses. Worshippers pray to them and often bring food as offerings for the dead and, on special occasions, fruits and flowers. Incense is always burning in temples to deliver messages to the heavens.

Ma-Tsu Temple, 30 Beckett Street. On the side street between Pacific and Jackson, this Taoist and Buddhist temple houses the Goddess Ma-Tsu, who looks after travelers and visitors. Unlike most temples, which require a challenging climb up several floors, Ma-Tsu provides easy access. Beautiful, red lanterns welcome visitors as they approach. Ma-Tsu, the Heavenly Mother (known as *Tien Hau* in Hong Kong), is a branch of the same temple in Taiwan, formally established in San Francisco in 1986. Its purpose is to advocate the virtues of Ma-Tsu: benevolence, upholding the spirit of the Buddhist dharma, teaching principles of human relations, and promoting social morality. As you enter the street-level temple, you are protected by the "all-seeing and all-hearing" dharma-protecting generals. Bright votive lamps in front of the various deities are located at the back center of the temple. Incense burns throughout the temple, with the smoke delivering messages to the heavens. Make a small donation and receive a talisman, blessed to protect you and yours.

Tien Hau Taoist Temple, 125 Waverly Place. Tien Hau is the Goddess of the Heaven and Sea, and her undying spirit remains active helping people in distress. Legend has it that Tien Hau (known as Ma-Tsu in Taiwan) was born with a heart full of good virtue and compassion, destined to be a savior of the mortals. She started to practice meditation at the age of eleven in search of truth and righteousness. The first Tien Hau Temple in San Francisco was built in Chinatown in 1852, which makes this temple organization one of the oldest in the United States. Be ready to go up three flights of steps to get to the temple.

Quong Ming Jade Emperor Palace, 1123 Powell Street. The Quong Ming Taoist and Buddhist Association is one of the largest in the United States. This temple started as one room in the mid-1950s and moved to its present location in 1994. Enshrined inside the Emperor's Palace is the Nam Mo Kwan Shi Yin Bodhisattva. Kwan Yin is very popular because she has a profoundly merciful heart of tenderness and the power to change calamity into prosperity. This palace's aims are to provide social services, cultural exchange, and to promote the Taoist way of life. The public is welcomed here, and often, Mrs. Mildred Fong, a dear woman and good friend, is present to welcome one and all.

On the first and fifteenth of each lunar month, the palace holds ritual ceremonies for peace, good health, and longevity. During the *Ching Ming* Festival, ceremonies are held to release the souls from purgatory and relocate ancestors from the hellish world to heaven and eternal peace.

Fook Chun Hall is a big room used for preserving ancestors' names, remembering dead relatives, and releasing dead souls from hell. The Master and Chanters of the Great Assembly pray to Bodhisattvas. The deity Yuen Ming Dow Low Tien Joon dissolves disasters of flood, fire, train wrecks, auto collision, mechanical failures in the air, and drowning at sea. He has fourteen extremely busy hands. The Kitchen God, Wang Ling Tin Goon (who wards off evil and cures sickness), the God of Happiness, the Earth God, the Door God, and other deities and immortals are here, too.

Kong Chow Temple, 855 Stockton Street. This temple, built in 1977, is atop the Chinatown Post Office. Located on the fourth floor, the temple is a large room that has a pyramid-shaped ceiling with a skylight. The beautiful altar showcases Kuan Ti with her attendant deities. Coincidentally, from its balcony, one can view the Transamerica Pyramid Building ... two Pyramid viewings for the price of one? The Kong Chow Temple is also the head office for the Kong Chow Benevolent Association.

Kong Chow Temple, above the U.S. Post Office, on Stockton Street.

Feng Shui

Feng shui (pronounced "foong zer," "fung shway," or "fung suey," depending on the dialect) is the ancient Chinese art of placement, to maximize your good luck in life and business. It is a way to manage *chi*, the flow of energy in all aspects of your environment.

The best way for me to begin this section about *feng shui* is to think back to when I first moved to my Wok Wiz office in San Francisco. I had the space for a wonderful ten years, and I believe that *feng shui* added to my happiness and success as a 654 Commercial Street tenant. When I first thought of moving my business into a space near Chinatown, I had several factors to consider. Foremost among them was a sense of connection. I walked around several blocks near the Financial District and Chinatown, and stopped in front of 654 Commercial Street because it simply felt right. I knew this building would be my new headquarters, even before setting foot into it. The building and I "connected." Another sign that this was the place for me was that the building faced south, and the address was numerically correct. The numbers 6, 5, 4, in that order sound like "good luck, no death." Sign me up!

Following are some key *feng shui* elements for a home, business, or office:

1. **Water at entryway.** Place a small fountain with running water atop a cabinet. The water is soothing and creates a relaxing welcome to your guests.

2. **Plants.** Potted plants represent growth and progress. Plants with rounded leaves are preferable because spiky leaves can create a hostile feeling in the environment. If you use cut flowers, promptly discard decaying blossoms to maintain a positive feeling.

3. **Wind chimes and crystals.** Wind chimes call in angels and eliminate negative energy.

4. **Mirrors.** Since mirrors reflect energy, *feng shui* experts place them to increase positive flow as well as to nullify negativity.

5. **Pictures and other hang-ups.** Mutual support is a positive *feng shui* force, and pictures remind us of the importance of family, love, and friendship.

6. **Art.** A painting of eight horses is always nice. The eight horses represent speed and power, and the number eight sounds like the word for prosperity.

7. **Couplets and colorful wall hangings.** Beautiful inscriptions, written on red paper, are displayed throughout the home, business, and office, especially during the two-week Lunar New Year period.

WOK WIZ'S RECOMMENDATIONS

Places to Sip Tea

Red Blossom Tea Company, 831 Grant. Peter and Alice Luong, a delightful brother-and-sister team, are experts on tea and give excellent narrations to our very interested Wok Wiz guests. Peter and Alice left their respective corporate careers to take over their parents' twenty-five-year-old business, and are doing a phenomenal job. The Red Blossom Tea Company is a direct importer, wholesaler, and retailer of premium teas and artisan tea ware from the Asian continent and around the world. This is a wonderful place for focus discussions on teas of your personal liking, and we encourage our guests to return after our tour to spend time with Peter and Alice or to learn more about rare and cherished seasonal teas. They are always enthusiastic to share their love for tea with you. www.redblossomtea.com

Above: Alice Luong, of Red Blossom Tea Shop, prepares fine tea for TV Chef Steffan Henssler, Hamburg, Germany, taping a show with Shirley.

Time for *Dim Sum*

Imperial Palace, 818 Washington Street. Ask for the Wok Wiz table, right in view of the *dim sum* chefs preparing fresh dumplings. Potstickers, Bean Curd Rolls, and Singapore Noodles are well executed.

Four Seas, 731 Grant Avenue. Located in the heart of Chinatown, Four Seas has a Hong Kong atmosphere, and offers tasty Cantonese specialties for *dim sum*, lunch, and banquets. www.fourseasrestaurant.com

City View, 662 Commercial Street. Close to Chinatown and the Financial District, this modern, well-kept dining room serves a wide variety of *dim sum*, as well as rice plates and noodle dishes.

Hang Ah Tea House, 1 Hang Ah Alley. On Sacramento, below Stockton. The oldest tea house in San Francisco's Chinatown, still frequented by loyal locals.

For SOMA (south of Market Street). Exquisite *dim sum* and more.

Yank Sing, 101 Spear (Rincon Annex). You must order the goldfish dumpling or rabbit dumpling just for the sheer fun of looking at them … then eat up these tasty steamed dumplings, filled with fresh shrimp and shaped into cute goldfish or rabbits. Maggie and Stella's favorites are the Sticky Rice in Lotus Leaves, Pan-Fried Tofu, Chicken Yee Mein, and Mango Pudding. Yank Sing is forever busy, so go early. A plus: discounted parking during the week, free parking on weekends. www.yanksing.com

Shanghai 1930, 133 Steuart Street. Transport yourself to the Shanghai 1930 era, in this gorgeous restaurant with a sexy lounge/bar. They have excellent food. If you want to eat in the bar, begin with a **Dim Sum** Steamer Trio. Enjoy complimentary jazz every evening. A couple of personal favorites: Yangtze River Lite Fry for its dramatic presentation and powerful flavors (tender white fish is lightly wrapped in river grass and flash-fried to perfection). Cindy's Chicken Claypot, Braised Five Spice Pork Shank, and for dessert, I suggest Sesame Profiteroles. They are similar to the traditional Sesame Balls … but these gems are filled with gooey, sinful Valrhona chocolate and another is filled with peanut butter. www.shanghai1930.com

You's, 675 Broadway. I recommend this for take-out *dim sum* or for *dim sum* on the street. I love their gigantic baked, or regular-sized steamed pork buns, and excellent snow pea tendril dumplings.

Eat like the Locals

Chef Hung's, 823 Clay. According to Frank Jang, this place has great Chinese "country-style" cooking.

Uncle's Café, 85 Waverly, corner of Clay. Very stark, filled in the mornings with regulars for coffee, breakfast, and lunch. It's cheap and good enough.

Capital, 839 Clay. Locals love to come here for tasty waffles and daily American specials. The Chinese need a getaway from their own food, and that is why you often see us diving into Roast Beef Rice Plate, or even spaghetti.

Yee's, 1131 Grant Avenue. Known for their roast pig and roast duck. The atmosphere is very authentic. Most of the chatter is in Chinese, as are the menus taped all over the walls. Noodles and rice plates are exceptional values here.

Yuet Lee, 1300 Stockton Street. It is packed with locals, often area chefs who come for Dungeness crab and fresh fish straight out of the tank.

Places for Casual Family Lunch or Dinner

Great Eastern Café, 649 Jackson Street. This attractive, neat restaurant gets good reviews for their seafood entrees, Chinese set dinners, as well as *dim sum* off the menu.

New Jackson Café, 640 Jackson Street. Nice, comfortable, and clean. Affordable American or Chinese style breakfasts, special lunch plates.

R & G Lounge, 631 Kearny Street. Freshly remodeled, the dining room is downstairs from the street-level lounge. Seafood is fresh, so order it Cantonese style, steamed with ginger and scallions, or try their popular Salt and Pepper Dungeness Crab. When in season, order a Steamed Crab.

Places for Northern-style Meals

Henry's Hunan, 674 Sacramento. Patriarch Henry Chung introduced spicy and hot Hunan food to San Francisco. Begin with Diane's Pancakes, then fire up your palate!

Hunan Home, 622 Jackson. The lunch crowd says it all. Be prepared to stand in line to get into this very-together restaurant. They have great food, excellent service, and the prices are easy on your wallet. Lily and James, the owners, often say, "Welcome home!"

Best Places to Buy Chinese Pastries

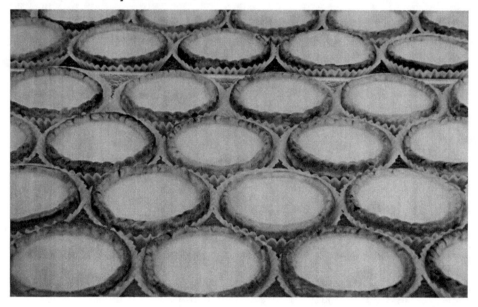

Egg Custard Tarts

Golden Gate Bakery, 1029 Grant Avenue. Fresh egg custard tarts and other traditional Chinese pastries.

Eastern Bakery, 720 Grant Avenue. Famous for mooncakes, snacks like "bow ties."

Dick Lee Pastry, 777 Jackson Street. Fresh egg custard tarts, lots of *dim sum* take-out.

Yong Kee, 732 Jackson Street. Only place in Chinatown that offers fresh Chicken/Pork/Chinese Sausage Buns. Say, what?

Best Places to Stay for the Lunar New Year's Parade

Hilton Hotel, Financial District, 750 Kearny Street, www.sanfranciscohilton-hotel.com. This beautiful new hotel is located directly across the street from Chinatown. Walk to the Financial District, North Beach, Embarcadero area, and downtown. There is complimentary wireless Internet in all guest rooms. Treat yourself to an award-winning Tru Spa treatment or two. Restaurant Seven Fifty is a bistro with fine dining. The lobby areas are sprawling and lovely, and the Hilton has one of the nicest front desk teams and friendly, helpful concierges. I love their Happy Hour treats, especially the house-prepared fresh pizza, fried calamari, and steamed mussels. My staff and I like to get together here to relax after conducting tours, with a cool drink and lounge food.

Above: Front row: Hank Quock, Shirley Fong-Torres; second row: Dorothy Quock, Howard Teng, Alberta Chinn, Lola Hom, Bernice Chinn, relaxing in the beautiful Hilton Financial District, 750 Kearny Street.

Mandarin Oriental, 222 Sansome. www.mandarinoriental.com/sanfrancisco. Go ahead and spoil yourselves; everyone deserves to spend a night or two at this exquisite hotel, just blocks from Chinatown and steps away from the California Street cable car line. Make reservations for a memorable dinner at Silks.

Orchard Garden Hotel, 466 Bush. www.sanfrancisco.com/orchard-garden-hotel. This beautiful boutique hotel is around the corner from the Gateway to Chinatown. It is California's first truly "green hotel." Each eco-friendly guest room is decorated attractively in calm colors and fabrics. The hotel has an in-room recycling system and uses chemical-free cleaning products.

Best Places to Buy Woks, Chinese Cleavers, Rice Cookers, and More

Ginn Wall Hardware, 1016 Grant. The oldest hardware store in Chinatown. Woks of all sizes, rice cookers, cleavers, knives, wonderful clay pots, Chinese dishes, bowls, even a pasta machine or two! Family-operated, friendly, and helpful.

Woks come in all sizes at Ginn Wall Hardware store.

The Wok Shop, 718 Grant Avenue. www.wokshop.com This is a small, but functional store filled with everything you need for your kitchen and gifts. You'll find woks, cleavers, cookbooks, and loads of Chinese cooking accessories. If you can't find it, owner Tane Chan will find it for you.

The Wok Shop

CHAPTER 15
MY FAMILY'S STORY

Memories of Angel Island

In 1910, the U.S. Immigration Service designated Angel Island, the largest island in the Bay, as a quarantine center for new immigrants. For Chinese, the name was bitterly ironic. They were detained there routinely for a few days, although in some cases it was for months or as long as two or three years. They were confined to their barracks and a small exercise yard. My mother was detained on the island and was one of the last residents there before the facility closed in 1940 following a fire.

The Immigration and Naturalization Service questioned "paper sons and daughters" for long hours about the details of their adopted families and villages. A few wrong answers could lead to immediate deportation. I greatly admire the courage of all the people who endured this to make a better life for themselves. Unfortunately, some people could not handle the stress and committed suicide rather than wait out the chance to land in San Francisco. Separated from their family and away from their homeland, many of the men and women could not deal with the misery of staying on the island. Others wrote poems of anguish and hope on the walls.

The story of my own family exemplifies how some Chinese gained entry to the United States with ingenuity. Both my father and mother came to America with purchased documents. My father was inspired by the success of other men from his village who found their way to America. He left China for Manila at the age of eighteen, in 1921. He worked for fifteen dollars a month, delivering bread. After six years in Manila, he was ready to move to America. Because the Philippines were a colony of the United States, he knew that he could enter as long as he carried a document indicating a Filipino name. For $1,200, he purchased papers that identified him as Ricardo Torres. Now he had a ticket to come to America; the year was 1927.

Upon his arrival, he was helped by the Fong Association, which assisted newcomers. He found a job washing dishes at the Fairmont Hotel on Nob Hill in San Francisco. Determined to do better, and since he enjoyed cooking, he took jobs that led him in that direction. When he heard that there were opportunities in Oakland, he went there. After working as a dishwasher, Dad soon became a cook and then a chef. By 1930, he had saved enough money to become a partner of New China restaurant in Oakland's Chinatown. Lunch was twenty-five cents, including salad, bread, coffee, and dessert. Years later, he opened another restaurant, New Eastern Café on Webster Street.

Relatives in China selected my mother as my father's bride. In 1940, as an eighteen-year-old, she journeyed to America to begin a new life. Her first impressions were dismal. Although it was a dream come true for her to come to the United States, she first spent over a month on Angel Island, a degrading and painful time. On June 26, 1940, my mother arrived in San Francisco, debarking from a twenty-one-day journey off the USS Cleveland. She was immediately transported to Angel Island, and remained there for forty-one days before she was freed on August 6. Father first saw my mother on the pier that day. Their marriage lasted fifty-one years, until his death. Mother told me, "When I first looked into Daddy's eyes, I saw a man with a kind heart."

In 2002, my mother and I returned to Angel Island, so that I could hear her story firsthand. She recalled the complex: "There was a big room with bunk beds, three levels each. Several tens of women lived in one room." While she waited weeks for her interview with the immigration service officials, Mother passed her time talking with others in the yard surrounding her living quarters. To this day, she calls it the prison. She was very frightened by the officers from the Immigration and Naturalization Services (INS) who quizzed her for several hours one day.

My mother explained, "I got along with the other people there, and they liked me because Father [her future husband] sent food from his restaurant three times a week. I shared it with my friends." A big box would arrive at 2:00 PM from our father, addressed to Mother. It was delivered to the kitchen. She had only a picture of my father up until that time, and knew that he was a good cook. The dish she remembers most, her favorite, was a braised fish stuffed with Chinese sausage, mushrooms, and water chestnuts. That may be another reason our mother was popular on Angel Island—who would want to vote her off the island when our father was sending such fabulous food?

Whereas my mother was very lucky to have food sent by Father, most detainees ate miserable food in the cafeteria. Dale Ching wrinkles his nose as he explains, "The taste was not the same as the way it should be. Mushy rice, *bok choy* that was cooked so long, the green vegetable became yellow. They counted the potatoes and carrots and made sure you did not take more than one. If meat was served, each person got roughly a two-inch piece, and don't ask for seconds."

Mother says that life there was like being in a cage. She would not use the bathroom without going with someone because she was afraid of ghosts. Many of the women were scared of the guards who might rape them. Some people hung themselves in the shower stalls.

"Once a week, we were allowed to go to a warehouse [where detainees personal belongings were stored] and pick up things from our suitcases." Mother smiles, "A nice woman, Katherine Maurer, a Methodist deaconess and assistant to missionary Donaldina Cameron, came to help us. She taught us English, gave us books and toys, sewing materials." The materials were donated by the San Francisco Bay Area Daughters of the American Revolution.

Dale Ching's Story

In 1937, at the age of sixteen, Dale Ching boarded the USS Hoover alone, headed to America to join the father he had never seen. His father had come earlier, and Dale's mother was to follow a few years later. That is how most Chinese families came to California, as parts of a whole seeking to be reunited.

In 2001, at age eighty, Mr. Ching was still volunteering his time as a docent on Angel Island. Encouraged by his grandchildren to return to where the family's American history began, he has often told his story to visitors. "I arrived in March, 1937. I thought I would see my father right away, that I was instantly a citizen. Instead, we were put on a boat and taken to Angel Island. Then I had to be interrogated."

Created by the Exclusion Act of 1882, the Detention Center on Angel Island became the "first stop" for all Asians coming into the United States. The California Gold Rush provided a great incentive for Chinese to pack their bags for America. Willing to work long hours for low wages, the Chinese were soon scorned, and the Exclusion Act passed through the U.S. Congress. It allowed entry only to those originally born in the United States, or to wives and children of citizens. Almost 175,000 Chinese immigrants passed through Angel Island, detained anywhere from two weeks to two years. Whereas Ellis Island, on the East Coast, welcomed immigrants to this country, Angel Island's goal was to exclude the new arrivals. For most former detainees, it is sorrowful and painful to return to Angel Island and relive their experiences.

"They tried to trick you in order to kick you out," Mr. Ching relates. "The interrogators separated husbands from wives, asked questions about your home and family, and if they didn't like your answer, or felt it did not match the set of answers they had, you were in fact detained longer or shipped back to China." For most detainees, Angel Island was a jail. Dale Ching remained on Angel Island over one hundred days. Having been interrogated, he then had to wait for the court to decide his fate.

Addressing a group of polite fifth graders from Antioch, California, Dale Ching tells how he arrived after a twenty-two-day journey, after his father said, "You are ready to go to America." He sighs as he tells about his "welcome party." Upon arrival, a group of armed guards with handcuffs, stood waiting on the dock. The immigrants were allowed to come onto the island with just what they had on, underwear, and a toothbrush. Most of the Chinese did not speak English, so they could only follow the guards and obey.

Their first stop was the hospital, where the men and women were separated and stripped down for physical examinations. "It was very embarrassing. And there was a guard watching, as if we were going to escape, naked. And, if you coughed at all, you could not go with the group, you had to stay behind."

Angel Island Detention Center included thirty-two buildings when my mother was held there. Now there are only two. Shattered foundations suggest the walls of my mother's jail: a main building, a two-story hospital, and a powerhouse. In the early days, it did not matter what country you came from; everyone passed through the Immigration Station—the Europeans, Indians, Japanese, Koreans, and Chinese.

Angel Island was named by the devil of deceit. There was nothing angelic about the barbed wired windows, tall fences, and sadistic armed guards that greeted immigrants. The rooms were small and crowded. One bathroom served the entire group, with no privacy. Many people carved poems on the walls of the barracks. Visitors can still see poems such as the following one, translated to English:

The way is far for the traveler;
Ten-thousand miles of difficult journey.
May I advise you not to sneak
across the border
The difficult and dangerous conditions are
not worth your curiosity.
These are not idle words
... written by one from Heung Shan

Segregated by race and sex, the immigrants spent most of their time in these so-called dormitories. A member of the San Francisco Housewives League (no date recorded) wrote, "The U.S. Immigration Station is just like a beautiful country home. It is surrounded by lawn, flowers, and trees. The station is a symbol of rest to the people who wait to enter the country." Chinese gamblers will lay you a million to one odds that no member of the Housewives League ever spent a night near any of the island's beautiful country homes.

Mother, at Angel Island's tribute to Trader Vic.

In a rare, sunny spot on Angel Island, my mother stood by a monument donated by the owner of Trader Vic's. Vic Bergeron was the original owner of an Oakland restaurant, Hinky Dink's, and he changed its name to Trader Vic's sometime around 1941. He was very friendly with the Chinese, and hired them almost exclusively at his restaurants. The monument that he carved thanked the Chinese immigrants for leaving their homes and villages for the Golden Gate. For my family, this monument represents angelic coincidence and the promise of America. In 1956, Dad became a chef at the first Trader Vic's, at 65th Street and San Pablo Avenue in Oakland. Trader Vic's restaurants blossomed, becoming very famous from San Francisco and Seattle to Honolulu and Singapore. In October, 2001, my good friend Gary Hirano opened the newest Trader Vic's, in Menlo Park, California.

In response to the carving, a plaque in the shape of a heart reads:

> *To Trader Vic,*
> *Our love, admiration and gratitude.*
> *Given this 28th Day of April, 1979*
> *At Angel Island Immigration Barracks.*
> *—By your Chinese American friends*

Angel Island Information:

Ferry Schedules
Tiburon-Angel Island Ferry Company (415) 435-2131

Blue and Gold Fleet (415) 773-1188

Angel Island State Park (415) 435-1915

John Soennichsen. *Miwoks to Missiles: a History of Angel Island* (Tiburon, CA: Angel Island Association, 2001).

Angel Island, now a state park, is one of the great under-utilized, historical landmarks of the Bay Area. It is often referred to as the "Ellis Island of the West Coast," a reminder to all that we are a nation of immigrants. Angel Island is accessible by ferry from Pier 41 in San Francisco and from Tiburon, but for over thirty years, it felt like a one-way ticket to fear and uncertainty, starting at the San Francisco port.

The museum at Ayala Cove will acquaint you with the history of Angel Island and the areas that you may want to explore. Of particular interest to most visitors is the North Garrison where immigrants, mostly from Asia, were detained and quarantined from 1910 to 1940, when a fire shut it down. The Chinese were detained there partially as a result of the tension created between them and other immigrants during the Gold Rush, when even the Exclusion Act of 1882 did not stop the Chinese from finding ways to get into America.

CHAPTER 16
THE EXCLUSION ACT

The great economic boom that many speculators expected to follow the completion of the railroad didn't happen. In fact, there were hard times throughout America in the 1870s. The railroad did make it much easier for unemployed workers from the East to come to California, which increased the competition for jobs.

By 1870, San Francisco had become the fifth leading manufacturing city in America. Chinese people held about half the jobs in manufacturing. The Chinese were different from other immigrants in that they thought of themselves as visitors rather than settlers, and they maintained close ties to their families and native villages. Most came with the goal of providing for their family in China, hoping to return to buy land or become merchants in China. They were willing to work endless hours at ridiculously low pay to achieve this goal.

In the 1870s, the Chinese became a convenient scapegoat for demagogues seeking political power who blamed the Chinese for taking jobs from non-Chinese workers. Several riots resulted in the burning of Chinese businesses. Some California cities, like Eureka, Truckee, Redlands, and Chico expelled all Chinese. San Francisco's Chinatown, like those in other cities, provided a refuge from violence and racism throughout the United States.

This anti-Chinese attitude led to the passage of the national Chinese Exclusion Act of 1882. Under the act, the only Chinese permitted to enter were foreign-born wives and children of American citizens of Chinese ancestry, or sons of men who had already established residence here. The Exclusion Act was strengthened and extended many times over the ensuing decades. The Immigration Act of 1924 removed even this right of wives and children. The Chinese are the only ethnic group that has ever been categorically excluded from coming to the United States.

The Exclusion Act has been called the "Extermination Act." It served its purpose well; from a peak of 132,000 in 1882, the Chinese population in the United States declined to about 62,000 by 1920. No doubt this decline would have been much more precipitous had it not been for the earthquake in San Francisco in 1906. Since all the records of citizenship for the western United States were destroyed in the firestorm that swept through San Francisco after the quake, it was difficult for the government to disprove Chinese claims to citizenship.

The Chinese did not passively accept the provisions of the exclusion laws. Like other ethnic groups, Chinese civic organizations fought legal battles for decades to achieve equality. By 1906, Chinese-born men were allowed to bring wives and children from China because of these legal battles. Men who returned to China often reported the birth of fictitious sons, creating a market in what became known as "Paper Sons," which enabled these younger men to come to the United States. But they were sons on paper only, and citizenship papers became a negotiable instrument. On December 17, 1943, President Franklin D. Roosevelt signed a law to repeal the Exclusion Act, a smart move to maintain good relations with China during World War II. It was the first time that our Chinese American men donned military uniforms and worked side-by-side with the Caucasian soldiers. However, the repeal was not satisfactory, because the quota for incoming Chinese was still very low. It was not until 1965 that the Exclusion Act was finally fully repealed, under the 1965 Civil Rights Act, opening the doors for thousands of Chinese immigrants.

Confession to Become Citizens

During the early 1950s, Chinese could acknowledge to the government that they were "paper sons" and become legal citizens. Dad did this so that each of his children could have a Chinese surname. However, he decided to remember the family that helped him gain entry into the United States, and he changed his name to Richard Fong-Torres.

Chinese are now on equal legal footing with other ethnic groups. Since 1965, there has been a great wave of new immigrants from Hong Kong, Taiwan, and other parts of China and Southeast Asia. Our San Francisco Chinatown is a bustling place that still gives newcomers a place to start in America, remaining a cultural oasis for thousands of Chinese Americans, as it has been for over 125 years.

In addition to the repeal of the Exclusion Act, the civil rights movement helped open up more opportunities for Chinese in the 1960s, expanding on the struggle for justice begun by pioneers in the Chinese community early in the century. Changes in the law made it easier to get results when fighting discrimination in education and business, and Chinatown had many activists who were involved in trying to get fairer treatment. The civil rights movement also helped reduce the pain of racial prejudice by making society appreciate the human dignity of all people.

Expanding opportunities in American society did not mean that Chinatown emptied. On the contrary, San Francisco's Chinatown saw a large increase in population after the Exclusion Act was fully repealed. Along with the growth in numbers, came the need for living space, jobs, and integration into American life. Earlier immigrants endured hardships and worked endless hours to make ends meet, but some of the younger, new immigrants were less patient and took issues into their own hands. While their parents found work wherever they could, some of these youth, who did not speak English and had a hard time adapting to American school and life, were not patient enough to start from the bottom up. Some chose to band together into gangs to make a living.

CHAPTER 17

"HE AIN'T HEAVY, HE'S MY BROTHER"

On June 27, 1972, the *San Francisco Chronicle* announced, "A brilliant and respected youth worker has become the tenth known victim in a series of Chinatown gangland slayings." There were reportedly two assailants. Two young men were stopped, driving around my brother's home, after the murder, but they were not arrested. Barry's case remains unsolved.

Our family was tragically and painfully caught up in those turbulent, changing times. All through the summer of 1972, I woke up listening to my all-time-favorite disc jockey, my brother Ben, on station KSAN. My most distinctive memory of his DJ days is still a cold Sunday morning, when he dedicated *He Ain't Heavy, He's My Brother*, to our eldest brother, Barry.

Barry was the executive director for the Chinatown Youth Center in San Francisco's Chinatown, on contract for one year starting in 1971. He had taken a leave of absence as a probation officer for the Contra Costa Probation Department, in Richmond, California to work in Chinatown.

The center opened in 1970 on Columbus Avenue, on the edge of Chinatown and North Beach. With the rise of Chinese gang wars and murders, it offered programs and services to work with potential delinquents and problem youths. The goal was to keep young people out of trouble by helping them through counseling, job placement, and self-help services. Barry was a dedicated social worker who knew the danger of his job.

I once offered to help Barry with one of his programs, but he said that it was not a good idea, that "if they want to get me, they may get you first."

My then-husband, Rich, and I had just returned from El Paso, Texas. We were far removed from the troubles in San Francisco's Chinatown. Our concerns had been the Vietnam War and getting through Rich's two years as an army officer at Fort Bliss. I taught physical education and English at Loretto Academy, a Catholic school for girls.

Barry wrote us regularly. In a letter in 1969, he joyfully told us about "bringing groups of youngsters from Richmond to the Ringling Brothers Circus, to the Cal Expo, and the California State Fair ... although it is a drain trying to keep tabs on twelve or more kids, especially very active acting out youngsters!"

Barry wrote, "As teachers, Shirley and Rich, you will both become very clear in your thoughts, as the need to transform loose random thought and knowledge into a coherent presentation makes everything clearer ... and when you realize that which you don't know, you'll want to fill the gaps through reading and research."

He wrote about his busy, full life, giving lectures at UC Berkeley on the effects of discrimination and segregation upon Chinese Americans, the evolution of Chinatowns, and racial stereotyping. He was a delegate for a governor's conference on children. In 1971, he visited Madrid to deliver a conference address on juvenile delinquency. I was eagerly waiting to hear about his time in Spain when I answered my sister Sarah's late night phone call. I still have trouble recounting the details.

Barry and his girlfriend, Gail, were playing Scrabble and listening to "A New Sound from the Japanese Bach Scene." The next day, June 26, Barry was to be a guest on KGO-radio, to talk about Chinatown's problems. An assassin intervened around 11:20 PM. The doorbell rang. Barry walked down a side alley to the front gate, where he was shot five times and killed.

Barry's death chilled my world, and rocked not only Chinatown, but our entire city. It devastated my parents, sister, brothers, relatives, and friends. Barry, Number One Son, was only twenty-nine. We attended UC Berkeley at the same time, and he was always there for me. He gave me the best advice about life and the world. He would come to my co-op to exercise with me, to make sure I stayed fit and healthy. I will never forget one of our talks when he advised me to "always reach out, read about things outside of your main interest, broaden your horizons."

Because I worked my way through college, Barry encouraged me to compete in a campus beauty contest, to win a partial scholarship. Only he could have given me the confidence to do so, and he came with my siblings to the Jack Tar Hotel to see me crowned as Miss Spring Informal, 1967. My parents were "too busy" at the restaurant, and did not come to the coronation.

Details of his life are clearer than those of his death. Barry suggested that I take a flight attendant job I was offered after graduating from Cal. He thought I was too young and immature to get married—that I should see the world, meet people, and experience life. It took many years, but I feel I now follow the path Barry encouraged me to take, and I did it because of him.

In one of our last conversations, Barry talked to me about our mother, who was making me angry over plans for my one-month-old daughter Tina's Red Egg and Ginger Party. I remember that afternoon, standing outside Mom and Dad's house on the porch. My wise older brother told me to just go along with our parents: they were not going to change. It wasn't about the party. Then Barry was taken from us. I miss him every day because I had a great brother who was a caring and wonderful man. I was especially sad that my daughter, Tina, would never be able to know her uncle.

After Barry's death, a part of me was drawn to San Francisco's Chinatown, where my brother worked to improve life there. And, even though my sister and brothers and I grew up in Oakland's Chinatown, I did not feel like an outsider. I warmed up to San Francisco's Chinese community immediately. Barry and I would have much to discuss if he were still with us.

At the time of Barry's death, the San Francisco Police Department had a small team of officers working the Chinatown gang detail. With rising crime, the police created the Asian Gang Task Force. The violence continued. In 1977, the Golden Dragon (restaurant) Massacre, a gang-related shooting, turned Chinatown into a ghost town for a long time, and I could barely go there. Thankfully, over the years, gang activity has subsided in Chinatown and it is a very safe place to visit.

In March, 2007, I was proud to represent my family at the 37th Annual Fundraiser for the Community Youth Center, the former Chinatown Youth Center. A few months before this gala, I closed down my Commercial Street office/cooking center, and it made complete sense to donate everything usable to CYC.

CHAPTER 18

DANCE OFF THE CALORIES— CHINATOWN'S NIGHTCLUB ERA

Forbidden City Nightclub and Other Chinatown Entertainment

In October 1997, I was proud to be an emcee for a benefit honoring the pioneers of the 1930s—1940s Chinese American nightclub era. The sold-out event was held in the Grand Ballroom of the Fairmont Hotel, where my father worked soon after his arrival in San Francisco. Father's spirit was very happy that my mother was in attendance. The fundraiser was for the retrofit and renovation of the former Chinese YWCA building, which now houses the Chinese Historical Society of America's National Chinese American Museum, at 965 Clay Street.

With the free time that the Chinese found after working long hours, many were drawn to the Chinese opera, music, and other forms of entertainment. Contrary to one of the stereotypes of Chinese, not everyone hung out in opium dens or gambled. In the 1930s and 1940s, Chinese and other Asian American performers broke into show business. Before long, the bars and clubs attracted tourists into the community, thus providing the Chinese with more jobs and opportunities. In 1935, Andy Wong, a trumpeter at the Grandview Tea Garden, took it over with his brothers and relatives, and gave it a new name.

Andy Wong's Chinese Sky Room became the first Chinese American nightclub in history, and was situated in a perfect location, on the corner of Grant Avenue and Pine Street. Today, it is the Grant Plaza Hotel. In 1936, Charlie Low and Collin Dong opened the Chinese Village cocktail lounge, followed by many others: Forbidden City, Club Mandalay, Kublai Khan, Shangri-La, and Lion's Den. Local author JoAnn Yuen's uncle Wilbert Wong was the owner of the 300-seat Club Mandalay, 720 Washington Street, from 1941 to 1947. It was a very popular club, for it offered lively floor shows, a ten-piece orchestra, singing, dancing, and food. In her childhood, Yuen practiced piano onstage at the Club Mandalay, and still performs with former Forbidden City vocalist Larry Ching.

Charlie Low opened the Forbidden City Nightclub in 1939. Located at 363 Sutter Street, it was the first nightclub of its kind, and created quite a stir from the very start. The nightclub featured Chinese Americans in song and dance, with a bit of burlesque thrown in. "Exotic" stereotypes of the Chinese were exploited, and the public flocked to the establishment. It was not commonplace to see the otherwise reserved Chinese people perform in this fashion. Larry Chan, the "Chinese Bing Crosby," Larry Ching, the "Chinese Frank Sinatra," and Toy Yat Mar, the "Chinese Sophie Tucker," and Paul Wing, the "Chinese Fred Astaire," and many other gifted entertainers attracted curious audiences.

My good friend, Joyce Narlock, has a direct connection: "My first memories are of the show kids (the performers). I met them first before my mom married Charlie. As I look back at all of them, they were really nice, fun people struggling to make a living, I think on fifty to seventy-five dollars a week. Many of the girls were single mothers trying to make ends meet. Some had jobs during the day as well."

Joyce was educated in boarding schools and private school, with no Asians around, which set her apart. When school was out, she lived in the adult atmosphere and grew up fast. She says, "It gave me some sophistication and a more comfortable feeling being around white people of some wealth. When the club was really busy, I was called upon to help as a hat-check girl, cocktail waitress, and cashier. Never mind that I was under-age!"

Joyce's childhood reminds me of my own, except that I grew up in a restaurant environment, not quite as colorful as hers! Joyce met movie stars such as Abbott and Costello, Vera-Ellen, Diana Lynn, Eddie Arnold, Gene Kelly, Bob Hope, and Annette Funicello.

Charlie Low has a reputation as being one of the most charismatic men of his time. In a documentary by Arthur Dong, *Forbidden City—USA*, Charlie is depicted as a great storyteller, a jokester, and a charming club owner who knew how to work a room. He always had a smile on his face and a hearty laugh, but was a savvy businessman. Always the center of attention, he loved to sing. His favorite was "Ragtime Cowboy Joe." He was loved by his customers, whom he treated like royalty. Though he was a tough boss, he always thought of his performers fondly as his show kids, his family. He was welcomed to the wealthy world of the "whites." His money didn't hurt because he had his own polo team, five polo ponies, and a race horse named Forbidden City.

Early on, Charlie Low was harness jockey for his race horses. This came naturally to him, having been born and raised as a cowboy in Winnemucca, Nevada. He was also an avid golfer who continued to play the game into his eighties. Low helped start the Chinatown Optimist Club, and was its first president. Joyce says lovingly, "When I was a young girl, I was asked many times, 'Are you Charlie Low's daughter?' by people with such a sense of awe in their voice. I couldn't understand, but now I do. I will always remember his song, his little dance, and his wonderful laugh." As a Chinese, he was truly one of a kind, a great example of courage to accomplish so much for the Asian community.

A Wok Wiz connection: Tour leader Chuck Gee was a young fashion designer for the Forbidden City performers. Today, he is still active in designing clothing for the "Grant Avenue Follies." Here he is with our San Francisco Mayor, Gavin Newsom.

CHAPTER 19
CLEMENT STREET
—THE "OTHER" CHINATOWN

An eclectic extension of San Francisco's Chinatown is the crowded and bustling Richmond District area simply called "Clement Street." It is often regarded as the "second" or "other" Chinatown, although it is not exclusively Chinese. Flanked roughly by Arguello (between Geary and California) and 25th Avenue, Clement Street is filled with ethnic businesses and restaurants. Visitors are encouraged to start their day here early, as this neighborhood is one of the most difficult for parking. We recommend public transportation. There is something for everyone here, from coffee houses, pizza, and an East European Deli, to donut shops, restaurants, herbal shops, and bars like O'Rourke's. When I need something spectacular to wear, I head over to 10th Avenue and Clement, to see my friends at Get Thee to the Nunnery.

Choose from a wealth of restaurants: Mai's Vietnamese, Burmese, Java Indonesian, Taiwan Restaurant, Guilin Garden at 291 6th Avenue, Wing Lee BBQ at 501 Clement Street, Narai (Thai) at 2229 Clement Street, or Le Soleil (Vietnamese) at 133 Clement Street.

Open markets tempt shoppers. The New May Wah Market at 547 Clement Street has two sections. I love their live tanks filled with fresh manila and geoduck clams, gigantic oysters, and swimming prawns and fish. Busy shoppers handpick tiger prawns, scallops, snails, and sea cucumber. The meat department offers nicely trimmed meats and good quality chickens. Next door, displays of fresh oranges, papayas, plums, and seasonal fruits and vegetables line the sidewalk. Inside are dried plums, ginger root, mushrooms, rice, canned goods, seasonings, and sauces. The New May Wah Market is a perfect stop to fill your Asian food pantry.

My food friend, Rhoda Wing, and I once went crazy at Kamei Restaurant Supply at 507 Clement. "We can go broke here!" Rhoda exclaimed, as we filled our carts with sushi platters, bowls, mugs, and realistic plastic replicas of Japanese food.

My favorite bakery on Clement is Shubert's on 6th Avenue. The popular bakery is operated by two brothers from Germany. They use fresh whipped cream and fruits for their scrumptious cakes, such as a Napoleon cake or Princess cake, and pies. Friends are still talking about my daughter Tina's engagement party cake from Shubert's.

Old and new book lovers can browse in Green Apple Books at 506 Clement. Further down is PPQ Vietnamese Restaurant on 25th and Clement, which features hearty bowls of *pho*, (noodle soup), or fresh Roast Crab with a side of Garlic Noodles, served with Imperial Rolls and Chicken Cabbage Salad. Stick around long enough, and the owner, Charlie Truong, will talk you into a karaoke singing match.

CHAPTER 20
MY HOMETOWN
—OAKLAND'S CHINATOWN

I grew up in Oakland's Chinatown where my parents owned the New Eastern Café, which later was renamed the Silver Dragon Restaurant. My brother, Ben, has written a family memoir about our lives there, *The Rice Room*.

Not only has Oakland's Chinatown drastically changed since we were children, but it differs significantly from San Francisco's Chinatown. One difference between the two is that, over the years, San Francisco has increased its effort to expand the tourism trade, while Oakland has remained focused mainly on the locals who live there. Another difference is more culturally distinctive, and disturbing to some Chinese. While San Francisco's Chinatown remains a tight Chinese, mostly Cantonese, community with sharp boundaries dictated by the financial pressures of expensive real estate, Oakland's Chinatown has expanded into a multi-national Asian community, with its demographics reflecting immigration trends.

The Vietnamese, Cambodian, Laotian, Filipino, Thai, Japanese, and Korean settlers have changed the face of Oakland's Asian community. Pacific Islanders, who now prefer to be distinguished from Asians, also have helped transform the community. This has not always been a smooth transition. In 2001, there were considerable accusations of racism when some Chinese groups resisted the name change of the Oakland Asian Cultural Center to the Oakland Asian Pacific Cultural Center. For the most part, the resistance was a media fire, based on anonymous flyers, but it drew attention to the pressures that come with changing times.

The corner of 8th and Webster has been the soul of Oakland's Chinatown since the 1870s. Two Chinatowns predated the one that grew here, but both were displaced by politics. One was moved so that a town hall could be built, the other because of high rents. Contrary to popular belief, Chinese settled in Oakland well before the railroads were built, and worked in the 1850s in tanning, flour milling, and wood planing companies. Other Chinese lived in the shrimp-boat camps here and north of Oakland. For several decades, the Chinese made up the entire population of Richmond, ten miles north of Oakland. Agriculture attracted more Chinese workers to the nearby land and then to the canning factories in Oakland. Temescal Dam and Lake Chabot Dam were built with exclusively Chinese labor in 1874—75 to supply the East Bay's drinking water. These early Chinese also made important contributions to California agriculture. They discovered that a hay grass grown for horses was edible asparagus when its green shoots were picked. Chinese also pioneered in using crop rotation systems, where multiple crops are grown on the same land and alternated for soil conservation.

In 1878, a traumatic event galvanized Chinatown. The Workingman's Party elected two racist leaders, J. H. and E. A. Redstone. These brothers based their politics on hatred and incited a riot against the Chinese at 8th and Webster. Violence, murder, and arson directed at the Chinese were common. By the time of the passage of the Exclusion Act of 1882, the Chinese had been terrorized out of the shrimp industry, and no canneries or agricultural employers would hire them, for fear of Workingman's Party reprisals. The only enterprise that employed Chinese workers in Oakland was the explosives industry, mostly because others did not want its dangerous jobs. Explosives remained the major industrial employment for Chinese workers until Giant Powder moved north to Point Pinole in 1912.

The second largest industry in Chinatown was gambling. *Fan tan*, *pai gow*, and *pak kop piu*, a numbers game that later became the casino game of Keno, was popular here among the bachelor society that grew up in a land where wives were not allowed to immigrate to join their husbands. This industry was independent and paid tribute to the police and politicians to remain so.

Oakland's Chinatown grew exponentially in 1906, when refugees from the San Francisco earthquake began crossing the bay. About four thousand Chinese were living here in Oakland's Lake Merritt refugee camp, segregated from others displaced by the earthquake. Oakland's Mayor Frank K. Mott encouraged the Chinese to stay in Oakland, beginning a bidding contest with San Francisco, which eventually capitulated and allowed its Chinese to rebuild their Chinatown on the same land as before. Still, some two thousand families stayed in Oakland's Chinatown, despite an offer from the Chinese ambassador for free passage back to China.

Some of the new Oaklanders included wealthy Chinese from the Six Families, the publisher of the daily newspaper *Chung Sai Yat Po*, the first Chinese dentist in Oakland (Charles Lee), and Lew Hing, the wealthiest Asian in America. By 1908, Chinatown extended from the water all the way to 10th street.

One of the more colorful characters in this period was Fong Yue. He built and flew the first airplane in California, in the Oakland hills, but later crashed another plane he built into his own factory. After that setback, he returned to China and led the aviation industry in his native country.

Lew Hing came to America in 1903 at age thirteen and began working menial jobs in the canning industry. By his twenty-first birthday, he had his own canning factory and a monthly payroll of $25,000. By 1920, he employed one thousand workers here and sold tuna and other products under the Buckskin label. He also owned steamships and mines. He died amidst economic ruin during the stock market crash of 1929, some say of suicide.

Another character who helped Chinatown grow was Joe Shoong, who founded the national Dollar Store chain. He moved to Oakland from Vallejo and headed his empire from Oakland while becoming a great philanthropist for Chinese American causes.

The 1920s were a decade of growth and isolation. All the,Chinese in Oakland lived in Chinatown, mainly because the U.S. Supreme Court upheld racist neighborhood covenants, which forbade selling property to Chinese. This discrimination backfired in one sense, because it galvanized the Chinese community. The Wakue School, first and largest in America was founded with Shoong's help in 1921, on the site where the Joy Luck restaurant now stands. The first Chinese Opera House in America was built on Webster, between 1st and 2nd Streets, in the 1920s.

In the 1920s, Washington Street, between 9th and 10th, became a butchers' retail area with a reputation for superior meats, and non-Chinese began frequenting the butcher shops. Shuck Yee, who went on to invent the peach pitter and the fortune cookie maker, came to Oakland in 1928 at age eight and attended the Lincoln School and later the University of California at Berkeley.

By the 1930s, Oakland Chinatown had become notorious. Besides the gambling industry, which by then had legions of white players, there was Fong Wan's nightclub, Shanghai Club, which stayed open most of the night. Fong Wan was a colorful character who was frequently arrested for practicing medicine without a license. He had so many patients that Western doctors often complained.

Everything began changing in the 1940s. The war brought shipbuilding jobs and prosperity to Oakland and Chinatown. With it came a new tolerance. By the decade's end, when the U.S. Supreme Court reversed its stance on restrictive covenants, Chinese began moving into other neighborhoods.

The following decades stand out for singular events that changed the look and soul of Chinatown. In 1954, gambling was closed down in Chinatown. In 1965, the U.S. Congress removed quotas on immigration from China; thousands came here from Guangdong (Canton) province, and later from Vietnam, Cambodia, Laos, Korea, and Thailand. The rush of multiple ethnic groups and a new liberalism in America changed the look of Chinatown from one of Chinese self-sufficiency to one more dependent on government services. Oakland's Asian population increased 51 percent between 1970 and 1980, and doubled by 1990, to make 16 percent of the total city population. Services such as child care, legal aid, library services, English language lessons, counseling, and welfare advisors replaced the family associations as the heart of the community.

Greater Chinatown in Oakland keeps growing, extending from Second Street to 12th Street and from the Oakland Convention Center on Clay to Oak Street. Asian stores blanket an even larger area, as far as 14th Street. This area borders the port of Oakland, and you can begin a walking tour of Chinatown at Jack London Square by walking north and east through the produce markets that offer the most exotic foods of Asia and South America.

Walking Tour of Oakland's Chinatown

The recent growth in the Asian population of Oakland comes from Southeast Asian countries. As you walk through Chinatown, you will notice many Vietnamese jewelry shops, restaurants, and markets. There are also many Cambodians, Koreans, and Laotians now living in Oakland and doing business in Chinatown. That is why I now consider it "Asiatown" rather than Chinatown.

The differences between San Francisco's Chinatown and Oakland's sometimes remind me of the theological distinction between "monkey grip" and "cat grip" salvation. Just as baby monkeys must hold on to their mother's back when fleeing a crisis, the San Francisco Chinatown community is based around family alliances and trade groups that try to make the community self-supporting. By contrast, the Oakland community has a large variety of government and nonprofit agencies and charities that can make immigrants less independent, like kittens carried from danger in their mother's mouth.

Oakland's Chinatown has a more modern, more American system of immigrant services. Government agencies are among the most visible tenants. The Asian Resource Center, at 317 9th and at 310 8th Street (it is an entire block long), houses groups like Sweat Shop Watch, Immigrant Women's Advocates, Asian Pacific Environmental Network, Asian Community Mental Health Center, East Bay Asian Local Development Corporation, Filipinos for Affirmative Action, National Network for Immigrant Refugee Rights, Adult Education Services and Classrooms, and Environmental Justice Fund. The building also showcases Asian American and African American artists in its hallways.

Other buildings are similarly large compared to those in San Francisco's Chinatown. Far East Commerce Plaza at 345 9th Street is home to the Language and Cultural Access Program, professionals of all kinds, World Books, and the Hop Lung Meat Market. The Pacific Renaissance Plaza was built in 1993 and contains 250 condominiums and apartments, with three underground parking levels. Its fountain courtyard is a perfect meeting spot. The Plaza houses the Public Library of Oakland and the Oakland Asian Pacific Cultural Center, where all forms of the arts are celebrated, taught, and exhibited—from classical *guzheng* (zither) playing to calligraphy to ballroom dancing to Filipino Hip Hop. The Kearney Street Workshop here nurtures the next generation of Asian American artists of all types.

The plaza also is home to myriad retail stores and restaurants. The popular 400-seat Restaurant Peony, on the mezzanine level, is very stylish and is home to many Chinese wedding banquets and large parties. They are always very busy, especially on weekends.

Another popular stop in the plaza is the Sweet Booth, on the ground level, where lactose-intolerant Asians learn the joys of ice cream. These days the use of exotic Asian fruits in desserts is quite popular: durian, lychee, and taro root ice cream, plus watermelon juice, red bean soy milk, slow-cooked papaya with agar, and the trendy tapioca pearl drinks.

The retail stores in Oakland's Chinatown sell as many Japanese crafts and cultural icons as Chinese and are geared to Asian buyers, not American tourists. The restaurants include sushi and Vietnamese cafes as well as *dim sum* and noodle shops. One of the best is Pho Hog-Lau, which offers the Cambodian *saifun* noodle. Le Cheval, at 1007 Clay Street, is a Vietnamese cafe specializing in lemon grass dishes and claypots.

My Favorite Chinese Restaurants

Yo Ho, 337 8th Street. It has live fish tanks filled with ling cod, rock cod, bass, geoducks, catfish, and crab. Yo Ho is bustling during the noon *dim sum* hour, so go early. I like their version of Thai Noodles, prepared with bean threads.

Chef Lau's, 301 8th Street, on the corner of Harrison. It features fish tanks and menus written in Chinese for the locals. They offer delicious dishes such as "live shrimp cooked two ways," which is a popular rendition of the "*yin yang*" cooking concept—either crisp with salt and pepper or poached whole shrimp.

Gold Medal, 381 8th Street. It is a great stop for duck dishes, dumplings, rice plates, and other Chinese deli items.

Joy Luck, 327 8th Street. It had that name for a decade before the publication of Amy Tan's popular novel. The Joy Luck serves wonderful rice plates and noodles at absolute bargain prices. Often, they offer delicious lobster *lo mein*.

Tin's Tea House, 701 Webster. It offers exotic dishes like ostrich in X.O. sauce and fresh geoduck clams and giant oysters, bigger than my fist.

Legendary Palace, 708 Franklin. It is making a name for itself with tanks filled with live fish, lobster, and crab, ordered and cooked on the spot. *Dim sum* is a big draw here, especially on weekends.

Points of Interest

Chao's Rosewood Furniture, on the corner of Harrison and 8th, features a big selection that cannot be easily found in San Francisco's Chinatown.

Sunshine Bridal & Photography at 324 8th Street gives a look at wedding finery in the Chinese style.

World Books, 628 Webster, features hard-to-find newspapers, magazines, videos, and CDs from all over Asia.

Tao Yuen Pastry, 816 Franklin, is notable for fresh *dim sum* dumplings, roast pork, and rice noodles.

The Chinese Community Center at 316 9th Street has not changed much from when my brothers, sister, and I attended Chinese language school there. If we were to become that age again, we would blend in just as we did years ago.

The architecturally splendid **Milton Shoong Building** at 316 9th is next to the bustling **Cheung Kong Supermarket**. Live fish and fresh seafood abound at the nearby **Harvest Fish Market**.

The Chinese Garden, which was completed in 1994, replaces the old Harrison Railroad Park at Harrison and 7th and is two blocks from the heart of Chinatown. Its pagoda-style structures can be seen from the Nimitz Freeway, guiding people to Oakland's Chinatown. At the entrance, two lion statues stand guard to protect all who enter. The Chinese Garden has a Chinese Pavilion and Pagoda, Memorial Hall, and a museum called the Hall of Pioneers. It has a reproduction of the famous nine-turn bridge that spans the West Lake in China.

The Light of Buddha Temple at 7th and Oak makes a peaceful end to any visit to Oakland's Chinatown.

More than one hundred thousand people visit the **Oakland Chinatown Street Fest** every year during the fourth weekend in August. There are cooking demonstrations and live entertainment. Vendors sell everything from ginseng roots, mushrooms, and soy milk, to T-shirts that say things like "Got Dim Sum?" to Asian music, purses, and even suitcases. Cultural performances show the talents of the community's many nationalities. Artisans sponsored by the Oakland Museum demonstrate arts and crafts of Asia. Some people come just to see the crowds and eat in the many stalls that serve Chinese, Vietnamese, Thai, and American food. For many years, my close friend, cooking teacher Rhoda Wing, was in charge of the Cook's Corner. For information, contact Oakland's Chinese Chamber of Commerce at 388 9th Street, Oakland, CA 94607, call (510) 893-8979, or see www.oaklandchinatownstreetfest.com.

CHAPTER 21

FAVORITE RECIPES FROM THE WOK WIZ

The following are simple recipes that have been requested by our Wok Wiz guests and my friends over the years. They are easy to follow, and ingredients are readily available in most food markets. I have included recipes for dishes that we eat on the tour as a part of our *dim sum* experience or for our food-centered "I Can't Believe I Ate My Way Through Chinatown!" Have a delicious time cooking!

BASICS
Homemade Stock
Homemade Potsticker Wrappers
Homemade Hoisin Sauce for Roast Pork, *Cha Sil*
Basic Fried Noodle Cake
Rainbow Fried Rice

APPETIZERS
Dad's Crab Rangoon
Tina's Onion Pancakes
Maggie's Hand-Hacked Seafood Potstickers
Bamboo Hut Spring Rolls

SOUPS
Turkey *Jook*—Rice Congee Soup
Lion's Head Soup
Fresh Watercress Soup
Corn Chowder, with a Chinese Twist

CHICKEN
Hand-Shredded Chinese Chicken Salad
Garlic Chicken with a Trio of Peppers
Lemon Chicken in a Claypot
Cashew Chicken with Snap or Snow Peas

VEGETABLES
Tofu Stir-Fry with Black Mushrooms and Snow or Snap Peas
Toasted Eggplant Curry
"I Love Vegetables" *Chow Mein*

SEAFOOD
Shanghai 1930s Salt & Pepper Crab
Steamed Whole Sand Dabs, Chinese Style

BEEF
Classic Asparagus Beef
Filet of Beef *Chow Fun*

Homemade Stock

Yield: 8 cups

2 or more pounds of pork bones
1 pound or more of chicken wings, back, thigh, carcass
A knuckle-size piece of fresh ginger, peeled, crushed
2 whole scallions, mash the white part, cut green part into 2-inch pieces
If available: peel of prawns (when you cook with prawns, save the peel, freeze and use later for stock)
1 whole yellow onion
1 whole carrot, cut into 2-inch pieces
2 large stalks of celery, chopped coarsely into 2-inch pieces
Sea salt
White pepper

Place all the bones and meat into a 2 ½-gallon stockpot. Fill with 16 cups of water, enough to cover all ingredients, bones and such. Bring to a near boil, and turn down heat and simmer for at least 6 hours. Let cool. Refrigerate the covered pot. The next day, skim off the fat before using in recipes. The stock should be gelatinous.

Notes:

1. If possible, use previously-baked bones and chicken—then you do not need to skim off fat the next day. Save bones from roasted chicken, vegetable discards to make a big pot of stock.

2. Make a batch to use in place of canned broth, although occasionally I like using packaged organic chicken broth.

Homemade Potsticker Wrappers

Makes approximately 30

If you cannot find potsticker wrappers in your neighborhood grocery store, it is fairly easy to make your own.

2 ½ cups of all-purpose flour
1/3 teaspoon sea salt
1 cup of warm water, may not need to use all

Bowl
Cutting Board
Food Processor

Place the flour and salt into the food processor bowl. Turn the processor on, and add water slowly down the chute. When the dough forms into a soft ball, remove and place on a lightly floured cutting board. Knead for approximately one minute, and form the dough into a ball, place in a bowl, cover with plastic wrap to rest for 30 minutes.

Lightly flour the cutting board again. Split the ball of dough into halves or thirds. Roll first ball into a cylinder, 1-inch in diameter, approximately 12 inches long. The rest of the dough goes back into the bowl, covered with a damp cloth.

Cut dough into 1-inch pieces. Use your hands to form each piece into a ball, and then use the side of a cleaver to form each wrapper into cute circles with approximately 2-inch diameters. You can also use a small rolling pin or your palms instead of a cleaver.

Place prepared wrappers on a lightly-floured plate, not touching one another, and continue making wrappers.

Homemade Hoisin Sauce for Roast Pork, *Cha Sil*

As an alternative to the bottled Hoisin sauce that is popular in roast pork and spareribs recipes, I developed this one, in an attempt to use less processed foods.

1–1 ¼ pound pork butt, cut into two strips, approximately 1 inch thick, 8 inches in length, set aside.

In a bowl, combine the following:

¼ cup tomato catsup
1 healthy size clove of fresh garlic, equally 1 teaspoon, finely minced
1 tablespoon packed brown sugar
1 teaspoon pure honey
1 tablespoon low-sodium soy sauce
½ teaspoon white pepper
1 green onion, green part only, finely minced
1 teaspoon rice vinegar
¼ cup Shao Xing wine or dry sherry

Marinade the pork for at least 6 hours, covered, in refrigerator.

Heat oven to 450 degrees. Bring down to 325 degrees and roast the pork on a rack (cover the bottom with aluminum foil for easier cleaning). Cook for approximately 45 minutes.

Basic Fried Noodle Cake

This is a fried noodle cake to use for *chow mein* dishes. Select your favorite noodles; I prefer the thin noodles, but the traditional ones are the regular-sized noodles.

1 pound fresh Chinese noodles
2 tablespoons vegetable oil

To cook: Bring 8 cups of water to a roaring boil. Place noodles in pot and stir around for ten seconds. Drain noodles in a colander and rinse with cold water. Rinsing the noodles prevents them from cooking any further and from sticking together. Set aside. Heat a 12-inch fry pan with oil, moving the pan around to distribute the oil. Add noodles to form a pancake. Fry noodles for 5 to 6 minutes. Check every few minutes to see if noodles are turning brown. Flip and cook other side. Add a small amount of oil to the side of the pan if the noodles stick to the bottom. Cook until the bottom side is golden brown. Remove to platter while rest of *chow mein* recipe is cooking.

The noodle cake can be prepared in advance and reheated when mixed in the wok.

Rainbow Fried Rice

This recipe is very much like the one my father used for his basic fried rice, served to thousands who came to our various Chinese restaurants. The trick is to be sure to use pre-cooked, cold rice. It should be rinsed and set to dry a bit before cooking. This will avoid the dreaded mushiness that can ruin rice. Also, I like to fry the egg, and add it back later. Or, if you want the rice to be moist, do not pre-cook the egg, but swirl it in when the rice is almost finished.

Serves 6 to 8

1 tablespoon vegetable oil
½ medium yellow onion, minced
1 cup of your choice, or combination of: diced Chinese roast pork, cooked ham, Chinese sausage, minced fresh prawns or scallops, cooked chicken, any leftover meat
4 cups cold, cooked long-grain rice (I suggest using leftovers.)
1 tablespoon soy sauce (low-salt preferred)
2 eggs, beaten, or 3 egg whites
½ cup frozen OR fresh (better) green peas
2 cups iceberg lettuce, shredded finely
½ cup minced green onion
1 teaspoon Asian 100% pure sesame oil
Sea salt
White pepper

To cook: Heat wok with oil, swirling to coat sides. Pan-fry the eggs until cooked. Remove. Reheat the wok, not adding any more oil. Stir-fry the onion until it turns translucent. Add choice(s) of meat or seafood and stir-fry over high heat for 2 minutes. Add rice and soy sauce and cook over high heat for another 2 minutes, mixing well. Add eggs or egg whites and cook for another minute. Add peas and lettuce and stir until lettuce cooks. Season with salt. Add additional soy sauce to taste, top with green onion, drizzle sesame oil, and sprinkle with white pepper.

Note: Use more or less of your favorite meat, poultry, or seafood. It's a great time to clean out your refrigerator. For vegetarians: use minced vegetables of your choice. Sometimes I add small cubes of tofu.

Dad's Crab Rangoon

Dad and his fellow chefs created this recipe at the original Trader Vic's. I think of my father whenever I prepare this.

Yield: 20 to 24

¼ to 1/3 pound crab meat (canned is fine, fresh is best)
¼ pound cream cheese
¼ teaspoon finely-minced garlic
1 teaspoon A-1, or other steak sauce
1 egg yolk
¼ teaspoon sea salt
1/8 teaspoon white pepper

24 *won ton* wrappers
3 to 4 cups of vegetable oil for deep frying
Hot mustard/soy sauce mixture, or your favorite cocktail sauce

Place the crab meat, cream cheese, and garlic in a bowl. Use a fork to mash everything together. Add the A-1 sauce and egg yolk. Sprinkle in salt and pepper.

Place a teaspoon of the filling on each *won ton* skin. Fold the corners over to form a triangle. Moisten the back corner of one edge and the front corner of another, twist until edges meet. Now you have a plump little crab Rangoon.

Heat the oil until very hot in a wok or deep fryer. Fry a few crab rangoons at a time until delicately browned. Drain on paper toweling. Serve with hot mustard/soy sauce, or your favorite cocktail sauce.

Tina's Onion Pancakes

This is a very simple recipe that my daughter, Tina, and I developed many years ago. We worked together to create a simple recipe with tasty results. Suggestion: use a non-stick pan to fry the pancakes.

Yield: approximately 20

2 cups all-purpose flour
2/3 cup hot water
½ cup minced green onions
½ cup sesame seeds
Extra all-purpose flour
1 tablespoon vegetable oil

Preparation: In a medium size bowl, mix flour with water. Knead for five minutes. Add green onions and sesame seeds. Divide and form into 2-inch balls. Place on lightly-floured board and use a rolling pin to roll out 5-inch flat circles.

To cook: Heat a frying pan with 1 tablespoon of vegetable oil, swirling to coat entire bottom lightly. Fry pancakes over medium heat until lightly brown on both sides. Repeat procedure with remaining pancakes, adding a little oil to the pan if needed. Remove from pan to a plate with paper towels to drain excess oil. Cut into quarters or sixths and serve as an appetizer.

Maggie's Hand-Hacked Seafood Potstickers

My granddaughter Maggie Sophia and I love making dumplings together. She started cooking with me at age two, and quickly became adept at wrapping the potstickers. For her fourth birthday lunch in 2007, Maggie chose to come home to make potstickers rather than go to a restaurant. This is a wonderful cooking project for you and the kids!

Yields: about 30

Have on hand: one pound of potsticker* wrappers (yield about 30), small bowl of cold water, 12-inch non-stick pan with cover, 2 cups of chicken broth.

1/3 pound each: lean ground pork or ground turkey, minced baby shrimp and/or bay scallops
1 cup of Napa cabbage plus 1 cup fresh spinach leaves
1 green onion, minced
3 cloves garlic, peeled and mashed
1 teaspoon fresh ginger
1 tablespoon soy sauce
½ teaspoon of Asian 100% pure sesame oil
pinch of white pepper

Filling: Chop by hand the pork, seafood, cabbage, spinach, green onion, garlic, and ginger. Place mixture into a bowl. Add soy sauce, sesame oil, and white pepper.

To assemble potstickers: Spoon 1 tablespoon of the filling into the center of each potsticker wrapper. Fold dough over to make a half-circle, moisten bottom half-circle with a small amount of water. Pleat edges firmly, forming 3—4 pleats on the top half-circle. Set each potsticker upright on a platter, so a flat base is formed.

To cook potstickers: Heat a 12-inch nonstick fry pan with 1 tablespoon oil. Place the potstickers close to one another. Brown the potstickers, about 30 seconds. Pour in enough broth to cover potstickers half way. Cover and cook over moderate heat for five minutes, until liquid evaporates. Use a spatula to remove potstickers carefully. Turn each potsticker over, dark side up, and place on a platter to serve.

Notes:

* Make homemade potsticker wrappers. See recipe at the front of this cooking section.

* I prefer purchasing *suey gow* wrappers if they are available. They are thinner and you can taste more of the filling.

* Have in little dishes an assortment of hot chili oil, vinegar, soy sauce, and sesame oil. Mix dip ingredients to suit individual taste.

* Use a non-stick fry pan instead of a cast iron pan because the non-stick fry pan requires less oil, and the potstickers slip out of the fry pan easily.

Bamboo Hut Spring Rolls

Spring Rolls, in some areas better known as Egg Rolls, are always popular with kids of all ages. I offer this recipe in remembrance of the thousands of Egg Rolls my brothers and I made at our restaurant in Hayward, California.

Yield: approximately 20

Have on hand: wok, strainer, 14-inch wok or pan for deep-frying

Filling:

1 cup shredded cooked ham or Chinese-style roast pork
1 cup shredded cooked chicken breast
½ cup minced prawns or cocktail shrimp
4 Chinese black mushrooms; soak in warm water for 10 minutes,
squeeze out excess water, remove stems, and mince caps
1 cup minced celery
½ cup minced bamboo shoot
2 cups fresh bean sprouts, rinse, drain, and dry with towels, then chop coarsely

1 tablespoon vegetable oil
3 cups vegetable oil for deep-frying
1 pound egg roll wrappers
1 egg, beaten (to seal egg rolls)
1 teaspoon cornstarch

Seasonings:

1 teaspoon sesame oil
1 tablespoon cornstarch
1 tablespoon low-sodium soy sauce
1 teaspoon sea salt
½ teaspoon white pepper

To prepare filling: Heat wok with 1 tablespoon of oil, swirling to coat sides. Stir-fry the filling ingredients for 3 to 4 minutes. Add seasonings. Remove from wok, place in a medium size bowl, cool for 20 minutes, and sprinkle with 1 teaspoon cornstarch.

Assembly: Place a heaping tablespoon of the filling in the center of a wrapper. Bring bottom of wrapper towards the top corner; bring sides together and roll. Seal with a little egg splash.

To cook: Heat a wok to 360 degrees with 3 cups of vegetable oil. Deep-fry the egg rolls for approximately 5 minutes, until golden brown. Drain on a rack, cool for 4 to 5 minutes. Cut into halves or thirds.

Suggestion for dips: Mix hot mustard with soy sauce, or hot mustard and cat-sup separately. I like to mix Japanese wasabi with low-sodium soy sauce.

Turkey *Jook*—Rice Congee Soup

Jook, also known as rice congee, is comfort food with a capital C. I grew up eating this, and it is still one of my favorites. It is great especially if the weather is cold, or if you have a hangover, or just do not feel good.

1 cup long-grain rice, washed and rinsed. To make it a creamier *jook*, change the proportions to ¾ cup regular long-grain rice, ¼ cup Arborio rice. Note: I experimented with brown rice and was pleasantly surprised at how tasty the *jook* came out.

2 turkey drumsticks/wings—approximate 2 pounds. Or, combination of drumstick/wings/legs/thigh. Bake in oven at 350 degrees for 1 ½ hours, remove meat, set aside. Use bones for the soup, and save the meat to return to the *jook* pot later.

1 quarter-size knob of fresh, peeled ginger
1 tablespoon sea salt
9 cups of water (or low-sodium chicken broth, or combination of both)
Optional, but a personal favorite: 4 to 6 bean curd sticks, *foo jook,* soaked in hot water until the sticks' color changes from yellow to a near white. Drain, cut into 2-inch pieces
Optional: gingko nuts, shelled, soaked in hot water and remove outer skin layer

Toppings, as desired: beat in 1 to 2 eggs right before serving, minced green onion, additional thinly julienned fresh ginger, minced fresh Chinese cilantro, white pepper, soy sauce, thousand-year-old egg, *pay donn* or preserved, salted egg, *hom donn.*

In a large stockpot, add the rice, turkey bones, ginger, sea salt, and water or chicken broth. Bring to a near-boil, lower the heat, cover the pot tightly, and simmer for 2 hours or more, until the rice has broken down and the soup is thick. Add more stock or water if the rice is too thick for your taste. During the last 30 minutes, add the *foo jook.* Transfer to serving bowls and have the toppings available.

*If you are using a crock pot, put it on LOW at night, and by morning, the *jook* is ready for you to add toppings to enjoy for breakfast.

Lion's Head Soup

I love this soup, which is hearty enough to be a meal. It is fun to make, delicious to eat. Meatballs represent the lion's head, the cabbage represents the mane, and bean threads represent whiskers.

Serves: 3 to 4

1 pound ground pork
1 whole green onion
1 teaspoon minced fresh ginger
1 teaspoon sea salt
2 tablespoons Xiao Sing rice wine or dry sherry
1 tablespoon vegetable oil
Chinese cabbage, cut off the end, separate into 8-10 whole leaves
1 quarter coin-size of peeled fresh ginger
1 star anise
4 cups chicken broth, homemade is recommended
2 ounces bean threads (Chinese vermicelli)
2 teaspoons minced green onions
Garnish: Chinese cilantro, remove stems

Have on-hand: a claypot or other casserole/soup pot

To prepare: Soak bean threads in hot water for 10—15 minutes. Drain and set aside. Chop the pork, green onion, and ginger together. Add salt, rice wine, and form pork into 4 meatballs.

To cook: Heat wok or pot with oil and lightly brown the meatballs. Drain and set aside. Using the same wok or pot, stir-fry the cabbage gently for one minute, season with a small amount of salt. Remove half of the cabbage leaves. Now, place ½ of the bean thread on top of ½ of the cabbage, and the meatballs on top. Add remaining bean threads next; place a quarter coin-size of mashed fresh ginger and break up, place the star anise in the middle of the pot, top with remaining cabbage. Add chicken broth and simmer for 30 minutes, until the meatballs are cooked and tender. Top with minced green onions and garnish with a flurry of Chinese cilantro. Roaring good!

Fresh Watercress Soup

Serves 5 to 6

3 Chinese black dried mushrooms
7 cups chicken stock (homemade is best)
4 cups of fresh watercress, remove and discard stems, chop into 2-inch pieces
1 teaspoon of peeled, minced fresh Chinese ginger
1 cup of firm tofu, cut into half-inch, bite-size cubes
1 egg, beaten
¼ pound of cooked chicken meat, sliced into toothpick sized strips
2 cloves garlic, chopped
1 teaspoon low-sodium soy sauce
Sea salt and white pepper, to taste

Soak the mushrooms in a cup of hot water or chicken stock for 15 minutes. Squeeze excess water or broth. Remove and discard the stems. Cut the caps into thirds or fourths. Place the remaining stock in a pot under high heat until it begins to bubble. Reduce heat and add watercress, mushrooms, ginger and tofu, cover and simmer for five minutes. Stir in the egg, chicken, and garlic and stir in an egg (the egg brightens the color of the broth). Remove from heat and season with soy sauce, sea salt, and white pepper. Serve immediately.

Corn Chowder with a Chinese Twist

I can still smell the corn chowder at the Bamboo Hut. I always looked forward to my father making it the Soup of the Day. Here is my version of that soup.

Serves 4 to 5

5 cups chicken stock
3 cups sweet corn in its own juices, grated or sliced from the cob (this can be cooked with a little salt and frozen for winter use)
1 stalk celery, chopped
1 green onion, chopped
1 teaspoon fresh ginger
½ teaspoon celery seed
Asian 100% pure sesame oil
Low-sodium soy sauce to taste
Sea salt and white pepper to taste
1 whole egg
6 sprigs fresh Chinese parsley (cilantro)

Bring stock to a near-boil. Add celery, onion, celery seed, and ginger. Reduce to simmer and cook 4 minutes.

Use a cleaver to remove corn kernels and their juice from cob. Be sure to scrape twice to get all the juice off the cob. Add to the stock and simmer two minutes. Whip the egg with sesame oil and soy sauce, gently add to the soup, stirring rapidly for about one minute.

Serve with sprigs of Chinese parsley (cilantro).

Hand-Shredded Chinese Chicken Salad

Note: This is an adaptation of my dad's "Hand-Shredded Chinese Chicken Salad." Rather than deep-fry the chicken, I roast it.

Have on hand:

12-inch wok, fill with 2 ½ cup vegetable oil, for deep-frying
14-inch wok for assembling the salad

One chicken, approximately 1 ½ pounds. Marinade for at least 2 hours in: ¼ cup low-sodium soy sauce, 2 teaspoons each of minced Chinese ginger and garlic, 1 teaspoon of Chinese five-spice (optional), and ¼ cup Shao Xing wine or dry sherry These days, you can save a lot of time and purchase delicious roast chickens in markets such as Mollie Stone's, Lunardi's, and Whole Foods.

2 ounces rice sticks (*mai fun*, found in most Asian food specialty markets)
2 green onions—mash white part lightly, cut entire green onion into half-inch pieces
1 tablespoon rice vinegar
½ head finely-shredded, fresh iceberg lettuce

½ cup unsalted peanuts, roasted to a golden brown, crush and set aside OR use pine nuts
1 tablespoon toasted sesame seeds
Your favorite salad dressing OR 2 teaspoons mixed Chinese hot mustard or wasabi, ¼ cup rice vinegar and ½ teaspoon pure sesame oil
1 bunch of Chinese parsley, rinse well, remove and discard stems

To prepare: Bake the chicken at 350 degrees until cooked, approximately one hour. Cool chicken. Remove the skin and bones, and shred the meat by hand. Toast sesame seeds in a small fry pan over medium heat, shaking gently, until golden brown. Set aside.

Putting the salad together: Deep-fry the rice sticks in first wok. Test the oil by placing one small piece of rice stick in the hot oil; if it puffs up, it is ready. Place small handfuls of the rice sticks into the wok. When the rice sticks puff up, remove from wok, and drain on paper towels. Heat second wok—do not add oil. Add the chicken, green onions, rice vinegar, and toss well. Turn heat off; add either the mustard and sesame oil mixture, or your favorite sesame oil salad dressing. Add the lettuce. Sprinkle the *mai fun* over the top of salad and toss again. Sprinkle with crushed nuts and sesame seeds. Top with a flurry of Chinese parsley.

Garlic Chicken with a Trio of Peppers

Serves: 2 to 3

1 whole chicken breast, skinned, boned, cut to bite size pieces. Marinade with:
      2 tablespoons soy sauce
      1 teaspoon of fresh minced ginger
      Dash of white pepper
      ½ teaspoon of sesame oil
      2 tablespoons Shao Xing (Chinese rice wine) or dry sherry

2 tablespoons vegetable oil
1 medium size yellow onion, peeled, sliced into thin pieces
8 cloves minced fresh garlic
¾ cup chicken broth
½ each: red, yellow, green bell peppers. Cut into halves, remove membranes and seeds. Cut each pepper into 1-inch bite-size pieces. *Use whole peppers if they are small
2 teaspoons low-sodium soy sauce
2 teaspoon cornstarch mixed with 1 tablespoon cold water
½ teaspoon hot chili oil (optional)
Asian 100 percent pure sesame oil or pure sesame oil with chili oil
Fresh sprigs of Chinese parsley (cilantro) for garnish

To cook: Heat wok with 1 tablespoon vegetable oil, swirling to coat sides. Stir-fry the onion and garlic until onion becomes translucent. Add chicken and trio of bell peppers. Stir-fry over high heat for 2 or 3 minutes, until chicken browns and bell peppers are cooked. Add ½ of chicken broth, bring to a boil and stir in the cornstarch mixture, to form a gravy. Drizzle with a small amount of hot chili oil (optional) and sesame oil. Serve immediately.

Top with parsley garnish.

*Substitute with other vegetables, such as broccoli, long beans, snap peas, your favorite!

Lemon Chicken in a Claypot

This version of Lemon Chicken is healthier than the typical recipe that uses deep-fried chicken and a sweet and sour lemon sauce. You can find claypots in stores like the Wok Shop or Ginn Wall in San Francisco, or perhaps kitchen supply shops.

Servings: 4

Have on hand:

2-quart claypot
Cabbage leaves to line claypot

1 chicken, approximately 2 ½ pounds. Cut to serving pieces; bone-in.
2 tablespoons vegetable oil

Blended mixture:
2 cloves garlic, minced
2 slices of fresh ginger, 1 inch by 2 inches, cut to matchstick size
1 teaspoon brown sugar
3 to 4 tablespoons Shao Xing wine or dry sherry
3 tablespoons low-sodium soy sauce
2 whole star anise
2 dried Chinese chili peppers
3 teaspoons of cornstarch mixed well with 2 tablespoons of cold water (will be used 2 separate times)

1 ½ cups fresh or organic chicken broth

1/3 cup fresh lemon juice
1/3 cup packed brown sugar

1 green onion, cut to 1-inch pieces

Preparation: Prepare blended mixture by putting all ingredients into a small bowl and mix well. Line claypot with cabbage leaves, and add ½ cup of chicken broth. In a small saucepan, combine lemon juice and brown sugar until sugar dissolves. Add ½ of the cornstarch mixture until the sauce is thick. Remove from heat and set aside.

To cook: Place wok over high heat until hot. Add vegetable oil, swirling to coat sides. Brown chicken pieces on all sides. Drain any fat and transfer chicken to the claypot that is lined with cabbage leaves. Add blended mixture. Mix well. Add chicken broth. Place claypot on range top, and raise heat gradually to a near boil, stirring gently. Cover and simmer over low heat for 35 minutes. Add the remaining cornstarch mixture. Stir in lemon sauce. Garnish with green onions. Bring claypot to the table to serve.

Cashew Chicken with Snap or Snow Peas

We love to prepare this at the start of the Lunar New Year as it promotes cash flow. First four letters of cashew are c-a-s-h!

Servings: 3 to 4

1 whole skinned chicken breast, sliced into bite-size pieces
Marinade for chicken: 2 tablespoons of dry sherry or Shao Xing wine, 1 tablespoon low-sodium soy sauce, and one teaspoon minced fresh ginger root

1 medium onion, peeled and sliced thinly
4 Chinese dried mushrooms, soaked in hot water for 10 minutes. Trim off stem; slice caps to thin matchstick pieces. Save soaking water to add to broth later.

4 fresh OR canned Chinese water chestnuts, sliced thinly (FRESH is highly recommended, or use jicama if that is easier to find)
2 stalks celery, sliced diagonally into thin pieces
¼ pound snap or snow peas, remove strings, rinse

½ cup chicken broth, homemade is recommended
1 tablespoon soy sauce
½ cup roasted cashew nuts
1 teaspoon cornstarch mixed well with 2 teaspoons cold water
1 teaspoon oyster sauce
1 to 2 drops of Asian 100 percent pure sesame oil
Optional: 1 to 2 drops of hot chili pepper oil

To cook: Heat wok with 1 tablespoon oil, swirling to coat sides. Stir-fry the prawns until they begin to turn pink, and remove to a bowl. Reheat the wok with another tablespoon of oil. Stir-fry the onion for 30 seconds. Add all vegetables except the snow peas. Stir-fry for 2—3 minutes. Season with soy sauce. Add chicken broth and liquid from mushroom soak. Return prawns to wok. Add the snow peas; stir in the cornstarch mixture, and mix together for a minute to cook the snow peas. Stir in the cashew nuts. Add oyster sauce. Remove to serving platter. Season with sesame oil and chili oil, if desired.

Tofu Stir-Fry with Black Mushrooms and Snow or Snap Peas

Fresh tofu is creamy white and very high in protein. It is usually sold in Chinese food markets, displayed on huge pans or in most markets in small containers. Use high-quality black mushrooms whenever possible; they taste much better. Serve this dish over rice. Add favorite green vegetables if desired and for extra color (e.g., broccoli or Chinese *bock choy*.)

Serves: 4 to 5

6 squares of firm (as opposed to silken or medium) tofu (approximately 3-inch cubes)
1 yellow onion, slice into thin pieces
2 cloves minced garlic
1 inch piece of fresh Chinese ginger, peeled and cut to matchstick slivers
8 Chinese dried black mushrooms, soak in hot water for 10 minutes, squeeze excess water, remove and discard stems, cut caps into halves
12 to 15 fresh snow peas, remove strings, leave whole
1 teaspoon low-sodium soy sauce
½ cup chicken or vegetable broth
1 teaspoon cornstarch mixed with 2 teaspoons cold water
1 whole green onion, minced
White pepper
½ teaspoon Asian 100 percent pure sesame oil

Heat wok with oil, swirling to coat sides. Stir-fry onion, garlic, ginger, and mushrooms for 2 to 3 minutes until the onion is translucent and garlic and ginger are fragrant. Add snow peas and stir-fry a minute. Fold in tofu and stir gently. Add soy sauce and chicken or vegetable broth. Bring to a boil, lower heat, and stir in cornstarch mixture. Add green onions, sprinkle with white pepper, and drizzle with sesame oil.

Toasted Eggplant Curry

This is my healthier variation of a dish I learned to make in Chiang Mai, Thailand, where it is usually made with coconut milk. Toasting eggplant is easy if you use the long, skinny eggplants (called by different names just about everywhere I travel). Hold them over an open flame by the stem or with tongs, or place them under a gas broiler. Turn them until all the skin is charred. Place the eggplants in a paper bag and cover for 5 minutes. Remove them from the bag and they peel easily. This is the best way to cook eggplants without using lots of oil.

Serves: 4 to 6

4 long skinny (Asian) eggplants, toasted
1 tablespoon sunflower oil
1 medium onion, chopped
4 cloves garlic, minced
1 jalapeno, seeds and membrane removed, minced
1 pound peeled, chopped tomatoes (canned is adequate when tomatoes are not in season)
2 teaspoons curry powder to taste
Chopped fresh coriander to taste

While eggplants are cooling in bag, heat the oil in a flat-bottom wok. Add the onion and jalapeno and sauté over low flame until onion is translucent.

Add the tomatoes with their juice, and curry. Stir well and cook over medium heat, covered, 10 minutes. Stir in the coriander.

Take the eggplants out of bag, peel and cut into one-inch pieces. Place the eggplant pieces on a plate and cover with the curry.

"I Love Vegetables" *Chow Mein*

This is a recipe that you can change depending on what is in your refrigerator; clean it out!

Serves 4

1 pound fresh Chinese egg noodles
2 tablespoons vegetable oil
1 medium size yellow onion, sliced into thin pieces
2 pieces of fresh Chinese ginger, approximately 1 inch by 2 inches, sliced thinly into matchstick size
8 Chinese dried black mushrooms, soak in hot water for 10 minutes; squeeze excess water, remove and discard stems, leave caps whole
½ cup cloud ears, soak in hot water for 10 minutes; drain, chop coarsely (optional)
½ cup minced green onion OR Chinese chives

1 pound total of assorted seasonal green vegetables of your choice, cut to bite-size pieces (e.g., *bock choy, baby bock choy,* long beans, Chinese turnip, Chinese cabbage, bean sprouts)

12 Chinese snow peas, remove tips and strings, leave whole

6 fresh or canned water chestnuts, cut into thin slices
1 tablespoon soy sauce
1 tablespoon oyster sauce
dash of white pepper
1 cup vegetarian broth
1 tablespoon cornstarch mixed well with 1 tablespoon cold water
½ teaspoon Asian 100 percent pure sesame oil
Garnish: Chinese parsley sprigs

To prepare noodles: Boil noodles in a large pot of water for 10 seconds. Rinse with cold water and drain well. Heat a 12-inch fry pan with 1 tablespoon of oil, swirling to coat entire bottom. Pan-fry noodles for 5—6 minutes until brown. Flip noodles and pan-fry the other side, adding more oil to the pan only if noodles appear to stick. Transfer noodles to a plate.

To cook: Heat wok with remaining tablespoon of oil, swirling to coat sides. Stir-fry onion, ginger, mushrooms and/or cloud ears, green onion or chives for a minute; add remaining vegetables and cook for several minutes, add soy sauce, oyster sauce, and vegetarian broth; sprinkle dash of pepper, bring everything to a boil and stir in cornstarch mixture. Return noodles to wok and mix everything together. Squirt in sesame oil. Top with a flurry of Chinese parsley.

Shanghai 1930s Salt and Pepper Dungeness Crab

I have had this dish numerous times. Forget about making it, just show up there!

1 fresh Dungeness Crab (approximately 2 ½ pounds)
1 tablespoon cornstarch
1 teaspoon chili, fresh, sliced
1 scallion, sliced
½ teaspoon salt and pepper, ground
1 teaspoon sugar, granulated
1 teaspoon rice wine
Pinch garlic, mashed
Pinch ginger, mashed
2 quarts peanut oil (save 2 tablespoons for stir-frying)

Preparation:

Clean the crab thoroughly. Remove the stomach and the gills. Then chop the crab into 6 pieces. Evenly coat the pieces with cornstarch.

Heat peanut oil in wok to 350 degrees. Deep-fry crab for 3 minutes, or until golden brown. Remove the crab and drain well.

Heat wok with 2 tablespoons of oil, until sizzling hot. Stir-fry the chili, garlic, and ginger for 30 seconds, or until slightly brown and aromatic. Then add the crab and stir-fry for another 2 minutes.

Then add the salt & pepper mixture, sugar and rice wine. Mix well. Cook for another minute. Serve hot.

Steamed Whole Sand Dabs, Chinese Style

Servings: 2 to 3

2 whole sand dabs or flounder, total approximately 1 ½ pounds

1 tablespoon low-sodium soy sauce
2 teaspoons Shao Xing wine or dry sherry
½ teaspoon sea salt
Dash of white pepper
Dash of Asian 100 percent pure sesame oil
¼ cup chicken broth

1 heaping tablespoon of thinly-julienned Chinese ginger
1 whole green onion, gently mash white part with side of cleaver, then mince the green onion (save 1/3 for garnish)

1 teaspoon cornstarch mixed well with a tablespoon of cold water

Thoroughly clean the fish, removing the head if desired. Lay the fish flat and cut into halves, place into a bowl and add the soy sauce, Shao Xing wine or dry sherry, salt, pepper, and sesame oil. Allow to sit for 10 to 15 minutes, place in a steaming plate, and add the broth (or water.)

Fill a 12-inch or 14-inch wok with enough water to almost reach the bottom of a steamer rack. Bring to a boil. Place the fish, which is in a heatproof plate, on the steamer rack. Be careful not to allow the water to touch the plate. Scatter ginger and approximately 2/3 of the minced green onion of top of the fish. Cover the wok, cook over medium high heat for about 10 minutes, until the base of the thickest part of the fish turns white.

When the fish is almost cooked, heat 2 tablespoons of vegetable oil in a small pan over medium heat. As soon as the fish is done, transfer to a serving platter, scatter the remaining green onion over the fish, and drizzle the hot oil on top.

Classic Asparagus Beef

Servings: 3 to 4

¾ pound flank or coulotte steak
        Marinade sauce:
        1 tablespoon soy sauce
        1 teaspoon minced fresh ginger
        2 tablespoons Shao Xing wine or dry sherry
        1 teaspoon cornstarch

½ pound fresh asparagus
1 tablespoon fermented black beans, rinsed; place in small bowl and add 2 cloves minced garlic and 1 teaspoon soy sauce

1 tablespoon vegetable oil
1 yellow onion, sliced thinly
½ cup chicken broth
1 tablespoon cornstarch mixed with 2 tablespoons cold water

Advance preparation: Trim fat from beef; slice against the grain into 1 ½ inches by 1 inch pieces. Place in bowl of prepared marinade for 10 to 15 minutes. Break off tough part of asparagus at the lower stem. Slice diagonally into thin pieces. In a small bowl, combine fermented black beans and garlic. Mash with the end of a cleaver to a paste. Add soy sauce and mix well. Prepare cornstarch mixture.

To cook: Heat wok. Add oil, swirling to coat sides. Stir-fry the asparagus for a minute. Remove and set aside. Re-heat wok without additional oil. Stir-fry onion, beef, and black bean sauce. Quickly, toss the asparagus back into the wok, and as you are stirring, add the broth and when the broth begins to bubble gently, stir in cornstarch-water mixture to form a light gravy. Serve with steamed rice.

Filet of Beef *Chow Fun*

This dish is often enjoyed on our Wok Wiz tour, at lunch. *Chow* translates to "stir-fry" in Cantonese, and *Fun* translates to "rice noodles."

Servings: 3 to 4

½ pound filet of beef or flank steak. Marinade in:
1 tablespoon Shao Xing wine or dry sherry
1 teaspoon fresh Chinese ginger, peeled, minced
Dash of sea salt and white pepper

1 tablespoon vegetable oil
1 pound of Chinese rice noodles (easy to find in Asian supermarkets)
1 yellow onion, slice thinly
½ cup of Chinese yellow chives, cut into 1-inch pieces (optional)
4 Chinese black mushrooms, soak in hot water for 10 minutes, squeeze excess water, remove and discard stem, cut caps into slices

2 cups Chinese snow peas, remove strings, leave whole
1 cup of fresh bean sprouts, if available
1 tablespoon soy sauce
White pepper to taste
Asian 100 percent pure sesame oil to taste
1 whole green onion, cut into half-inch pieces

To cook: Cut rice noodles into strips to approximately ¾ inches wide. Heat wok with oil, swirling to coat sides. When smoky, add onion, yellow chives, mushrooms, and beef. Cook over high heat until fragrant, about 30 seconds. Add snow peas and bean sprouts, stir-fry another 2—3 minutes. Add noodles, a handful at a time, and soy sauce, stirring to mix everything together. Season with white pepper and sesame oil. Top with green onions.

NOTE: rice noodles can be made at home, but it is much more convenient if you can find them in an Asian food specialty store, or an Asian pastry shop.

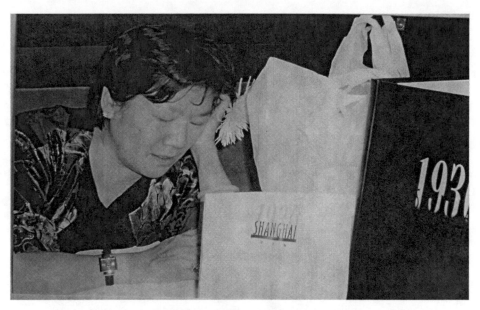

The Wok Wiz ate so much, she dozed off. "I can't believe I couldn't eat everything." Good thing Shanghai 1930 offers doggie bags. Woof, Woof!

ABOUT THE AUTHOR

Shirley Fong-Torres grew up in Chinatown, in Oakland, California. Shirley's parents operated Chinese restaurants, and her mother worked in sewing factories nearby. After her graduation from the University of California at Berkeley, Shirley taught Language Arts and Physical Education in Texas and California. She worked at Levi Strauss in San Francisco for eight years and her last position was *Operations Manager, Merchandising, Womenswear Division.* Her love of people and Chinese cooking, along with her interest in Chinese American history, eventually merged. Shirley left the corporate world to form her company: Wok Wiz Chinatown Tours & Cooking Co., and has operated her business since 1984.

Shirley is the author of three books and is a freelance food and travel writer. She appears on national and international television and radio shows. She travels often to Hawaii to appear as a guest chef, judge cooking contests, speak on panels or to film for Hawaiian Airlines in-flight videos. Shirley resides in the peninsula, near San Francisco. She is the proud mother of Tina Dong Pavao and mother-in-law to sports fan Matthew Pavao, and is a loving grandmother to Maggie Sophia and Stella Olina. In her spare time, Shirley cooks and gardens with her granddaughters, dances to rock 'n' roll music, goes to baseball games all over the country, and pretends to know how to shoot pool. Shirley's next goal is to learn how to play the guitar.

For more information about Shirley's Wok Wiz tours and programs, please visit her website, www.wokwiz.com or email her at shirley@wokwiz.com.

BIBLIOGRAPHY AND RECOMMENDED BOOKS

Chin, Wee Yeow, and Hsuan Keng. *Chinese Medicinal Herbs.* United Kingdom: CRCS Publications, 1992.

Chinn, Thomas. *A History of the Chinese in California.* San Francisco: Chinese Historical Society of America, 1969.

Chinn, Thomas. *Bridging the Pacific.* San Francisco: Chinese Historical Society of America, 1989.

Dobie, Charles Calwell. *San Francisco's Chinatown.* New York: D. Appleton-Century Co., 1936.

Farkas, Lani Ah Tye. *Bury My Bones in America.* Nevada City: Carl Mautz Publishing, 1998.

Fong-Torres, Ben. *Rice Room: Growing up Chinese-American—from Number Two Son to Rock 'n' Roll.* New York: Penguin Books, 1995.

Jan, Lyle. *China 2227 Long, Long Ago.* West Conshohocken, PA: Infinity Publishing.com, 2006.

Lai, Him Mark. *Becoming Chinese American: A History of Communities and Institutions.* Landham, Maryland: Altamira Press, 2004.

Lin, Henry B. *Chinese Health Care Secrets.* MN: Llewellyn Publications, 2000.

Martin, Mildred Crowl. *Chinatown's Angry Angel.* Palo Alto, CA: Pacific Books, 1977.

McCunn, Ruthanne Lum. *An Illustrated History of the Chinese in America.* Design Enterprises of San Francisco, 1979.

See, Lisa. *On Gold Mountain.* New York: Vintage Books, 1996.

Stevens, Keith. *Chinese Gods*. London: Collins & Brown, 1997.

Takaki, Ronald. *Strangers from a Different Shore*. Boston: Little, Brown and Company, 1989.

Wong, William. *Oakland's Chinatown*. San Francisco, CA: Arcadia Publishing, 2004.

Yan, Martin. *Invitation to Chinese Cooking*. San Francisco, CA: Bay Books, 1999.

Martin Yan's Feasts. San Francisco, CA: KQED Books, 1998

Yung, Judy and the Chinese Historical Society of America. San Francisco, CA: *San Francisco's Chinatown*. Arcadia Publishing, 2006.

ACKNOWLEDGMENTS

The last twenty-plus years on Planet Wok Wiz have been delicious. I meant to write this book five years ago, but life's adventures kept getting in my way.

I present my fourth book, written with the encouragement of important people in my life. Besides a loving family, I have many close and dear friends, colleagues, and new, happy relationships with friends in the world of writing, radio, TV, restaurants, and hotels.

I thank our father, who worked hard all his life and still maintained a great sense of humor. I applaud our mother, Connie, for her bravery in coming to this country to marry our father, and together, they had five children. I am blessed with a loving and devoted daughter, Tina Dong Pavao, who keeps me semi-organized in and out of my office, and for bringing her girls, Maggie and Stella, to cook or garden and play with me. Tina is a fourth-grade teacher, and still manages to help me out. To Matt, my son-in-law, with whom I spar over Fantasy Baseball—go, Giants! It is with loving memories of big brother Barry that I write this book—his time in and contribution to the Chinese community is one of the reasons I started my Wok Wiz business. I always look forward to spending time with my sister, Sarah, and her husband, Dave; my brother Ben and his wife, Dianne; and brother Burt. My niece, Lea, and her husband John are now parents to little Haden, and my nephew, Jason, will soon marry his lady, Wendy. To Jim Duncan, who is as constant as the northern star—he always cheers me on and gives support even 1,500 miles away. He is the best researcher, a top-notch writer who possesses a witty sense of humor and gives me ideas that light up in my brain. I appreciate the many hours that he has contributed to help me get this book written.

To Tane Chan, energetic, hard-working owner of The Wok Shop, who practically begged me to get my book published and directed me to these two ladies: Joy Elliott and Melissa Dalton of iUniverse. Joy and Melissa held my hands as I gingerly entered the world of self-publishing, and I am ever grateful to Tane for that push. Much appreciation to my wonderful friends Kenny Wardell, who photographed this book cover and back cover, and contributed a few pictures within, and to Frank Jang, a good guy, always ready to help out in the community with his camera—ready to snap pictures at a multitude of events. Frank spent countless hours with me to place pictures in my book.

It is a joy to work with Scott Sorensen, of Coco Palm Pictures, to put together in-flight videos for Hawaiian Airlines. I thank Steve Chin, who designed and watches over my Web site, www.wokwiz.com, to Jeanne Francis, my publisher at Steppin' Out, and George Medovoy, my editor for postcardsforyou.com.

I have been a member of the San Francisco Convention & Visitors Bureau for well over twenty years, and am delighted to be a member of its various committees, as well as serve occasionally on its Board of Directors. Being a member of the Bureau was one of the first and smartest moves I made as "Wok Wiz." I am also involved with the Chinese Historical Society, the Chinese Culture Center, as well as the hospitality programs at San Francisco State University and the University of San Francisco.

Thanks to Ross Rumsey, my "cyber friend" that I have yet to meet face-to-face, although we have been IM-ing since 1996. Ross has been very supportive of my projects over the years, and produced one of my Wok Wiz promotional tapes. He is a producer/director/announcer for ABC/Disney—KFSN-TV in Fresno, CA. I hope to meet Ross and his wife, Bobbi, perhaps at a book-signing?

My Wok Wiz walking tour business keeps on rockin', thanks to the best team of tour leaders I could dream for. I still enjoy leading the tours, but cannot conduct them all by myself. I rely on my very intelligent, fun-loving A-Team. I met Bernice Fong when I was a guest on a PBS cooking show. This gracious woman is a recipe developer, and she made my food look good on-air. Dorothy Quock, a "save the precious panda" campaigner, enchants our guests with her Chinatown stories. Alberta Chinn and I love to talk about restaurants, shopping, and our grandchildren. She has great ideas for dining and trips, so do pick her brain. Chuck Gee is such fun to be with. He was one of the original fashion designers for the Forbidden City Nightclub and still designs clothing for entertainers. He spent over twenty years working in the catering department of the San Francisco Hilton. Hank Quock was born in Chinatown, was a caterer, cooking teacher, and former president of the Association of Chinese Cooking Teachers. Hank also works for the Department of Motor Vehicles. Howard Teng is a Cardiologist Technologist, and in 2007 received an award in Washington, D.C. He is now a Fellow of the Society of Nuclear Medicine. Lola Hom works for the United States Department of Education, and on weekends she charms visitors on our walking tours. Lola makes you feel right at home in our Chinatown. Judy Won is a fourth-grade teacher in San Francisco, and we are happy she can help out on occasional weekends. My dear friends, Rhoda Wing and George Mew, though retired, are two original Wok Wiz tour leaders, and Madeline Sherry set up our first office. I also thank Larry Mak, Ophelia Wong, Cynthia Yee, Lily Smith, and Russell Chinn for their years of outstanding service adding to the success of our company. New York days are made brighter by Scott Newman, president of Zerve (www.zerve.com). We greatly appreciate the wonderful service that Scott and his team provide in booking our tours.

In July 2007, I cared for my one-year-old granddaughter, Stella, for three days. I set up an itinerary for her as if she was on a press trip. I came to the realization that I was either nuts, really serious about my work as a food and travel journalist, or both. I am very appreciative of the hard work that my public relations friends put into setting up fabulous press trips. Thank you, Debbie Geiger—you and your team open up the world to me, and I am always thrilled to write about the people and destinations you introduce to me. Mahalo to my friends at the Oahu Visitors Bureau, Maui Visitors Bureau, and Kona Visitors Bureau for their friendship and assistance over the years.

The Media has been very kind to me. Thanks to our local TV and radio shows for inviting me as a guest: Joey Altman's *Bay Café*, Liam Mayclem's *Eye on the Bay*, and *Dining Around with Gene Burns*. I do shows for the Food Network, Travel Channel, Fine Living Channel, PBS, Discovery Channel, History Channel, Good Morning America, the TODAY show, and Fine Living. It is great fun to appear on the *Bobby Flay Show, Rachael Ray Show, Unwrapped, Ready, Set, Cook!*, the Burt Wolf travel show, comedian/actor Mark DeCarlo's *A Taste of America*, and Martin Yan's cooking shows. Internationally, it was a thrill to work with Chef Steffen Henssler of Hamburg, Germany, as well as Martin Clune and Keith Floyd of the UK, Dorinda Hafner of Australia, ITV-London's *Wish You Were Here*, INDIA-TV, Amsterdam-TV, French-TV, Travel Channel - Passport in San Francisco with Samantha Brown, and so many more, I cannot keep track.

With great delight, we have led tours and done cooking shows for companies such as Google, LeapFrog, Oracle, Bon Appetit, Dreamworks, Les Dames D'Escoffier, Grantmakers for Education, Torani, IBM, Tauck Discovery Tours, Chevron, Amex, Torani Italian Syrups, Collette Vacations, Campbell Soup, Air France, Wells Fargo, *Maxi* magazine, and Smith Barney.

Comedian Mark DeCarlo, star of A Taste of America, *Travel Channel. We taped in Chinatown and had a "Chop Suey Cook-Off" at Shanghai 1930.*

Many schools and colleges have supported Wok Wiz over the years, and we are happy to be a part of the students' understanding of our people, history, culture, and food. We strive to make a positive impact on their lives. Some of the following schools and colleges have been coming to tour with us for many years, and others are our new friends: Hoover School, Redwood City; Stone Lake Elementary School, Elk Grove; Cabrillo School, Pacifica; Pioneer School, Gateway School, Santa Cruz; Franklin High School, El Paso, TX; Half Moon Bay High School, Charles Armstrong School, Brookfield Academy, Urban Promise High School, Lower Lake High School, Healdsburg High School, Lawson Middle School, Bellarmine College Preparation School, Leonardo da Vinci School, Mercy High School, San Francisco; and Davidson College, North Carolina.

Above: Chicken Feet? All right! Justin and Jonathan Sam, and Julius Raval, sixth-graders at Cabrillo School.

978-0-595-44867-8
0-595-44867-4